NAVY AIR COLORS

United States Navy, Marine Corps And Coast Guard
Aircraft Camouflage and Markings
Vol. 2 1945-1985

Thomas E. Doll
Berkley R. Jackson
William A. Riley

illustrated by Don Greer
and Kevin Wornkey

Squadron/Signal Publications

F3H-2 Demons of VF-131 off USS CONSTELLATION in the colorful markings common to the late Fifties.

ISBN 0-89747-168-7

If you have any photographs of the aircraft, armor, soldiers or ships of any nation, particularly wartime snapshots, why not share them with us and help make Squadron/Signal's books all the more interesting and complete in the future. Any photograph sent to us will be copied and the original returned. The donor will be fully credited for any photos used. Please indicate if you wish us not to return the photos. Please send them to: Squadron/Signal Publications, Inc., 1115 Crowley Dr., Carrollton, TX 75011-5010.

DEDICATION

To that largely anonymous group of amateur photographers whose documentation of the planes, the people, and the places constitutes an invaluable contribution to the history of aviation.

ACKNOWLEDGEMENTS

We are deeply indebted to the following individuals for their assistance during the preparation of this work. Included are some of the finest and most respected names in the field of aviation history. These dedicated gentlemen gave of their time and resources to make this book possible.

Special mention must be made regarding the extra effort and contribution of the following five men. Our project could not have started without them.

Harold Andrews
Harry Gann
Rowland P Gill
William T Larkins
Arthur Schoeni

Mention must also be made of the fine contribution of time and energy given co-author Doll by Randall L Robb. An eighteen month tour of Vietnam veteran, Randy always came through in true Marine Corps style when needed. "*Semper Fi*, Randy."

A special "thank you" to Jerry L Campbell of Squadron Signal Publications for his patience and to Don Greer for his excellent artwork. And thanks to the staff at Squadron Signal for their outstanding courtesy.

To all the others... Thank you very much...

George Adair
Peter Bergagnini
John W Caler
Bunny 'd E C Darby
Clifford W Doll Jr
Bude Donato
Fred Drinkwater
Major John Elliot, USMC, Ret
Bob Ferguson, Lockheed California Company
Keith Ferris
A W Frascella, Naval Air Systems Command
Ariel L Go
R T Gralow, Northrop
Clay Jansson
Stan Kalas
Duane Kasulka
Jerry Kishpaugh
C E Krischano
Robert L Lawson
Eric Lundahl
Gregory Nikola
Cdr H S Packard, USN, Ret
Lee Pearson
NAS Pensacola Photo Lab
LCdr J M Pierce, USNR
Harrison Rued
Capt W E Scarborough, USN, Ret
Jim Sullivan
Douglas R Tachauer
Philip A Tachauer
Edward L Torres
USCG Public Information Office
USMC Historical Branch
D Bruce Van Alstine
Gordon S Williams
Roy J Wills Jr
Hideki Yamauchi

INTRODUCTION

Documenting post-WW II United States Navy and Marine Corps aircraft colors and markings proved somewhat less difficult than compiling Volume One in this series. Since we are dealing with a time period much closer to the present day photographic documentation is more extensive than during the 1920s and 30s. Cameras and film were increasingly easier to obtain and there were more opportunities to photograph military aircraft, not only during the many air shows presented over the last forty years, but also thanks to such organizations as the American Aviation Historical Society, the International Plastic Modelers Society and the Tailhook Association, there has been more open access to the various Naval and Marine Corps Air Stations across the United States.

As in Volume One, we have endeavored to present as complete a picture of the subject as we were able to obtain. There are certain documents on markings that we know exist but were not available to us during the preparation of this volume, these are listed in the text. However, in the main, Volume Two presents a very complete picture of its subject. We thank you for your support of Volume One and hope Volume Two adds to your knowledge and enjoyment of United States Navy, Marine Corps and Coast Guard color and markings.

POST WAR YEARS

World War Two became history, fancy marking schemes gave way to the simple alphabet system introduced and found so very satisfactory during the closing weeks of WW II.

The lettering code issued in July of 1945 was changed on 8 January 1946 when Commander Air Force, Pacific Fleet issued a letter, **F39, FF12-5/(15-on), serial 093**, recommending that the letters be changed around as a form of updating the system. Some carriers did use the letters recommended in this letter, however, it is not known if all the Fleet carriers used the letters assigned. While the directive ordered the letters applied to the tail section of the aircraft, as they had been in July 1945, at least a few applied the letter symbols to the side of the aircraft.

Identification letters assigned were as follows:

USS Saratoga (CV-3)	MM	USS Antietam (CV-36)	A
USS Ranger (CV-4)	BB	USS Princeton (CV-37)	P
USS Enterprise (CV-6)	EE	USS Shangri La (CV-38)	X
USS Essex (CV-9)	E	USS Lake Champlain (CV-39)	Z
USS Yorktown (CV-10)	Y	USS Tarawa (CV-40)	T
USS Intrepid (CV-11)	HH	USS Midway (CVB-41)	M
USS Hornet (CV-12)	FF	USS Franklin D Roosevelt (CVB-42)	F
USS Franklin (CV-13)	S	USS Coral Sea (CVB-43)	C
USS Ticonderoga (CV-14)	TT	USS Valley Forge (CV-45)	V
USS Randolph (CV-15)	R	USS Philippine Sea (CV-47)	H
USS Lexington (CV-16)	LL	USS Independence (CVL-22)	DD
USS Bunker Hill (CV-17)	U	USS Belleau Wood (CVL-24)	RR
USS Wasp (CV-18)	XX	USS Cowpens (CVL-25)	CC
USS Hancock (CV-19)	N	USS Monterey (CVL-26)	AA
USS Bennington (CV-20)	SS	USS Cabot (CVL-28)	UU
USS Boxer (CV-21)	B	USS Langley (CVL-27)	PP
USS Bon Homme Richard (CV-31)	KK	USS Bataan (CVL-29)	VV
USS Leyte (CV-32)	L	USS San Jacinto (CVL-30)	YY
USS Kearsarge (CV-33)	K	USS Saipan (CVL-48)	ZZ
USS Oriskany (CV-34)	D	USS Wright (CVL-49)	W

Enclosures with this letter included a diagram detailing the proper positioning of the tail and wing letters and their size. Double letters were to be 30 inches in height and single letters were to be 36 inches high.

Aircraft numbers for fuselage and wings were assigned in blocks by type of aircraft and squadron.

Fighters	**(VF) - 101**	to	**199**
Fighter-bombers	**(VBF) - 201**	to	**299**
Scout-bombers	**(VSB) - 301**	to	**399**
Torpedo	**(VT) - 401**	to	**499**

The numbering within blocks was to be consecutive. Commander Air Group (CAG) planes could be marked 100, 200, 300, 400 according to the type of aircraft assigned.

The squadron insignia could be applied to the fuselage at a point approximately 12 inches forward of the fuselage number and 12 inches below the cockpit rim extended. The squadron insignia could not exceed 6 inches in diameter.

A note at the end of the letter stated that the dimensions given in the diagram may be modified to allow the letters and numerals to best conform to the surface on which they were applied, providing the modification did not defeat the purpose for which the system was devised. That being the quick identification of US Navy aircraft.

Photographic evidence from 1946 indicates that for a short period of time carrier-based aircraft carried a horizontal stripe across the top portion of the rudder and vertical stabilizer, similar to the marking used by Air Group 15 during 1944. This 1946 application appears to have occurred only on the East Coast of the United States, but that is merely conjecture. The only photo viewed by the authors shows SB2Cs and F4Us of Air Group 75 from the USS FRANKLIN D ROOSEVELT (CVB-42). The tail stripe on the SB2Cs carry the squadron designation VT-75 in what appears to be White lettering and the stripe itself appears to be Red in color. The F4U's stripe is Yellow or White and carries VF-75 in Black. The authors are positive a directive covering this marking was issued during that time period but at this writing such a document has not surfaced.

On 6 May 1946, **Amendment -3** to **SR-2e** was issued. This amendment outlined the paint scheme for Target Towing aircraft. The scheme for single engined target towing aircraft was as follows:

Glossy Orange Yellow:
- Wings - top and bottom of all airfoil sections.
- Vertical fin - horizontal stabilizer and elevators.

Glossy Sea Blue:
- Fuselage and cowling - Wing walkways - on both sides of fuselage, extending 18 inches outboard on topside only of wings.

Glossy Insignia Red:
- Rudder -
- Wing bands - around both wings. Three feet wide, centerline parallel to thrust line at one-third distance from fuselage to wing tip.

The scheme for multi-engined aircraft was as follows:

Glossy Orange Yellow:
- Wings - top and bottom of all airfoil sections.
- Vertical fins - horizontal stabilizers and elevators.

Glossy Sea Blue:
- Fuselage -
- Engine nacelles and cowlings - except those portions included within topside of wing planform.
- Wing walkway - on both sides of fuselage, extending 18 inches outboard on topside only of wings.

Glossy Insignia Red:
- Rudders -
- Wing bands - around both wings. Three feet wide, centerline parallel to thrust line and midway between insignia and outboard nacelle.

General Motors TBM-3E Avenger of Torpedo Squadron 20 (VT-20) during 1946. Pre-WW II style coding appears on fuselage and underside of port wing. This practice was followed mainly by stateside units and continued into the immediate post-WW II period. Some examples were photographed in combat zones during WW II, but these were the exceptions not the rule. Coding is Insignia White and was applied to the top surface of the starboard wing also. The Avenger is painted overall Glossy Sea Blue. (Harry Gann)

Vertical fin fairings shall be painted Glossy Sea Blue. Terminate Glossy Orange Yellow on a line formed by projecting the fin leading edge down to the fuselage.

Sea Blue wing walkways may be eliminated from aircraft whose crews do not walk on the wings to enter the plane. When applied, they shall extend from extreme leading edge to trailing edge of wing.

In the event of insufficient space for Red wing band between insignia and nacelle, locate band adjacent to nacelle, parallel to thrust line. Insignia may overlap. Do not cover or alter insignia size or location.

On 6 June 1946, a revision to **ANA Bulletin No 166** of September 1943 made its appearance. The notable changes in this bulletin, **166a**, were the redesignation of color names in use since before WW II. True Blue became Light Blue, Willow Green became Light Green, and Lemon Yellow became Light Yellow.

On 10 June 1946, **Amendment 1** to **Army-Navy Insignia Specification, AN-I-9b** was issued. This order called for the discontinuance of the Insignia Blue outline and circle in the application of the US national insignia when applied to backgrounds of Glossy Sea Blue or Black. This practice was common to Grumman F6F Hellcats before the end of WW II, but not to aircraft of non-Grumman manufacture. The 10 June directive made it mandatory on all USN aircraft with the aforementioned color schemes.

An addition to **ANA Bulletin No 157, ANA Bulletin 157b**, was issued on 20 August 1946. This bulletin designated additional colors for use on USN aircraft should the need arise.

In late 1946, the most ambitious of all the tail letter identification markings directives was issued. On 7 November 1946 **Aviation Circular Letter No 156-46** came down to all ships, stations and units concerned with aircraft operations. The letters G, Y, J, N, O and Q were eliminated, since they were considered to be ambiguous characters by the Chief of Naval Operations. The contents of **ACL 156-46** were as follows:

Carrier Squadrons

(a) Letter-numeral system.
(b) Letter(s) assigned to carrier groups signified the parent carrier.
(c) 3-digit block numeral system was assigned by type and squadrons. The sequence VF-, VF-, VA-, and VA- was used and the squadrons were assigned blocks of numbers thus:

VF-squadrons 101-199 VA-squadrons 301-399
VF-squadrons 201-299 VA-squadrons 401-499

The numbering of aircraft within squadrons and the blocks were numbered consecutively. Commander Air Group (CAG) aircraft were marked 100, 200, 300, 400, according to the type of aircraft assigned.

Patrol Squadrons - VP
Photographic Squadrons - VPP
Weather Reconnaissance Squadrons - VPW
Meteorological Squadrons - VPM
Utility Squadrons - VU
Transport Utility Squadrons - VRU
Experimental and Development Squadrons - VX
Night Composite Squadrons - VCN

(a) Letter-numeral system.
(b) The first of two letters designated the wing or class. The second letter designated the squadron within the wing.
(c) The planes within a squadron were to be numbered consecutively starting with the number ONE.

Fleet Aircraft Service Squadrons (FASRONS):
(a) Letter-numeral system.
(b) Markings consisted of the last three digits of the individual aircraft's Bureau number.

Training Command:
(a) Letter-numeral system.
(b) The first of two letters designated the base or station. The second letter identified the squadron and/or the class designation.
(c) One, two or three digit numerals were used to number the planes within the squadons. The numbers were to be consecutive.
(d) The Chief of Naval Air Training controlled the assignment of the letter symbols within the Training Command. This assignment could be delegated to the various Functional Training Commands.

Naval Air Transport Service (NATS):
(a) Numeral system.
(b) NATS planes used their bureau numbers for individual aircraft identification.

Marine Squadrons:
(a) Carrier based squadrons used the letters assigned to their parent carriers. Tail and wing letters on USMC planes were to be underscored to designate USMC.
(b) Land-based squadrons used two letters for their identification. The first letter designated the Wing or Command and the second letter designated the squadron within the Wing or Command.

(ABOVE) SB2C-5s and F4U-4s of Air Group 75 with horizontal bands on their vertical tail surfaces. Color of bands appears to be Insignia Red on the Helldivers and either Insignia White or Light Yellow on the Corsairs. Carrier is USS FRANKLIN D ROOSEVELT (CVB-42) in mid-1946. (USN)

COMMANDER AIR GROUP 17 (CAG 17) Stanley W Vejtasa in his Vought F4U-4 Corsair at Brunswick, Maine in 1946. Coding is Insignia White with aircraft color being Glossy Sea Blue. (Stan Kalas)

Carrier Air Groups were also given new designations according to their assigned carrier. Four types were designated. They were:

CVBG	**for**	**Battle Carrier**
CVG	**for**	**Attack Carrier**
CVLG	**for**	**Light Carrier**
CVEG	**for**	**Escort Carrier**

Carrier squadrons were limited to Fighter and Attack Squadrons. The designations VBF, VB and VT were eliminated. The fighter and attack squadrons were given suffix letters to indicate their carrier type assignment*.

Squadron redesignations were as follows:

A for Attack Carrier Air Group

From	To
VF-3	VF-3A
VF-4	VF-1A
VF-5	VF-5A
VBF-4	VF-2A

B for Battle Carrier Air Group

From	To
VF-17	VF-5B
VF-18	VF-7A
VF-19	VF-19A
VF-20	VF-9A
VF-74	VF-1B
VBF-74	VF-2B
VBF-3	VF-4A
VF-75	VF-3B
VBF-75	VF-4B
VBF-5	VF-6A
VBF-17	VF-6B
VBF-18	VF-8A

E for Escort Carrier Air Group

From	To	From	To
VF-42	VF-2E	VT-75	VA-4B
VF-82	VF-17A	VB-5	VA-5A
VBF-20	VF-10A	VT-5	VA-6A
VF-98	VF-221A	VB-17	VA-5B
VF-11	VF-11A	VT-17	VA-6B
VBF-11	VF-12A	VB-18	VA-7A
VF-81	VF-13A	VT-18	VA-8A
VBF-81	VF-14A	VB-20	VA-9A
VF-153	VF-15A	VT-20	VA-10A
VBF-153	VF-16A	VB-11	VA-11A
VBF-82	VF-18A	VT-11	VA-12A
VBF-19	VF-20A	VB-18	VA-13A
VB-4	VA-1A	VT-81	VA-14A
VT-4	VA-2A	VB-153	VA-15A
VB-74	VA-1B	VT-153	VA-16A
VT-74	VA-2B	VB-82	VA-17A
VB-3	VA-3A	VT-82	VA-18A
VT-3	VA-4A	VB-19	VA-19A
VB-75	VA-3B	VT-19	VA-20A

Additional Squadrons

From	To	
VF-41	VF-1E	Decommissioned 9-1-48
VF-58	VF-1L	L for Light Carrier Air Group Decom. 11-20-48
VF-98	VF-21A	Decommissioned 8-5-47
VBF-98	VF-22A	Decommissioned 8-5-47
VT-41	VA-1E	Decommissioned 9-1-48
VT-58	VA-1L	Decommissioned 11-20-48
VB-98	VA-21A	Decommissioned 8-5-47
VT-98	VA-22A	Decommissioned 8-5-47
VT-42	VA-2E	Redesignated VC-22 9-1-48

** History of Naval and Marine Fleet Aviation Unit Designations from 1 June 1941 to 15 December 1948.*
Op331B/jfs
A12-1
Serial: 1694P33

Curtiss SB2C-5 Helldiver in the torpedo bombing role. The squadron is VT-17 operating out of NAS Norfolk, Virginia during 1946. Fuselage coding is Insignia White, the aircraft Glossy Sea Blue. The pilot is Ensign Stanley Kalas. (Stan Kalas Collection)

Marine Corps Northrop F2T-1 Black Widow night fighter in a well worn overall Glossy Black finish. Still carrying the Army Air Force serial number, this is one of five P-61 fighters turned over to the Marine Corps after WW II, and used for training at MCAS Miramar, California. (USMC)

(Below) The beautiful "4 by 2" in overall Glossy Sea Blue. The PB4Y-2 Privateer featured an Engineering and Research Company (ERCO) bow turret and ERCO 250TH waist blisters. All lettering on this Privateer is Insignia White. (William A Riley)

Assignment list of letter symbols for USN aircraft per ACL No 156

USS MIDWAY (CVB-41)	M
USS F D ROOSEVELT (CVB-42)	F
USS CORAL SEA (CVB-43)	C
USS RANDOLPH (CV-15)	R
USS BOXER (CV-21)	B
USS LEYTE (CV-32)	L
USS KEARSARGE (CV-33)	K
USS ORISKANY (CV-34)	RI
USS ANTIETAM (CV-36)	A
USS PRINCETON (CV-37)	P
USS SHANGRI LA (CV-38)	S
USS TARAWA (CV-40)	T
USS VALLEY FORGE (CV-45)	V
USS PHILIPPINE SEA (CV-47)	PS
USS SAIPAN (CVL-48)	SA
USS WRIGHT (CVL-49)	W
USS SALERNO BAY (CVE-110)	SB
USS SIBONEY (CVE-112)	SI
USS RENDOVA (CVE-114)	RE
USS BAIROKO (CVE-115)	BA
USS BADOENG STRAIT (CVE-116)	BS
USS SAIDOR (CVE-117)	SR
USS SICILY (CVE-118)	SL
USS POINT CRUZ (CVE-119)	PZ
USS MINDORO (CVE-120)	MI
USS PALAU (CVE-122)	PA

FLEET AIR WINGS AND THEIR SQUADRONS*

Fleet Air Wing 3		C
VP-MS -10	(ex-VP-74)	CA
VP-ML -3	(ex-VP-136)	CB
VP-MS -4	(ex-VP-204)	CC

Fleet Air Wing 5		E
VP-MS -9	(ex-VP-19)	EA
VP-AM -3	(ex-VP-71)	EB
VP-AM -4	(ex-VP-73)	EC
VP-ML -5	(VP-135)	ED
VP-MS -5	(ex-VP-205)	EE
VPP-2	(ex-VD-2)	EF
VPM-3	(ex-VPW-3)	ER

Fleet Air Wing 11		M
VP-MS - 1	(ex-VP-201)	MA
VP-MS - 8	(ex-VP-208)	MB

Fleet Air Wing 1		A
VP-MS - 11	(ex-VP-21)	AA
VP-HL - 8	(ex-VP-128)	AB

Fleet Air Wing 2		B
VP-MS - 7	(ex-VP-27)	BA
VP-HL - 13	(ex-VP-115)	BB
VP-HL - 3	(ex-VP-124)	BC
VP-HL - 5	(ex-VP-143)	BD
VP-ML - 6	(ex-VP-146)	BE

Fleet Air Wing 4		D
VP-AM - 1	(ex-VP-53)	DA
VP-AM - 2	(ex-VP-62)	DB
VP-HL - 7	(ex-VP-107)	DC
VP-HL - 10	(ex-VP-120)	DD
VP-HL - 12	(ex-VP-122)	DE
VP-AM - 5	(ex-VP-5)	DF

Fleet Air Wing 7		H
VP-HL - 4	(ex-VP-104)	HA
VP-HL - 6	(ex-VP-114)	HB
VP-HL - 11	(ex-VP-111)	HC

Fleet Air Wing 10		L
VP-MS - 3	(ex-VP-28)	LA
VP-HL - 9	(ex-VP-119)	LB

FLeet Air Wing 14		S
VP-MS - 2	(ex-VP-22)	SA
VP-ML - 2	(ex-VP-130)	SB
VP-ML - 4	(ex-VP-144)	SC
VPP - 1	(ex-VD-5)	SD

Fleet Air Wing 18		W
VP-MS - 6	(ex-VP-32)	WA
VP-HL - 2	(ex-VP-102)	WB
VP-HL - 1	(ex-VP-116)	WC
VPM - 1	(ex-VPW-1)	WD

*VP-MS *(Medium Seaplane Squadron)*
VP-ML (Medium Patrol Squadron)
VP-HL (Heavy Patrol Squadron)
VP-AM (Amphibious Patrol Squadron)
VPP (Photographic Squadron)
VPM (Meteorological Squadron)
Redesignation of VP to VP-MS, etc., made 15 November 1946.

BATTLESHIP AND CRUISER SQUADRONS

(VO) BAT SPOT RONS

VO-1B	BA	VO-2B	BB

(VO) CRU SPOT RONS

VO-1C	CA	VO-13C	CE
VO-2C	CB	VO-15C	CF
VO10C	CC	VO-17C	CH

USMC SQUADRON LETTER SYMBOLS

FIRST MARINE AIRCRAFT WING

HEDRON (Headquarters Squadron MAW-1)	A
VM0-3 AA VMO-6	AB
HEDRON MAG (Marine Air Group) 24	**AD**
VMF-115	AE
VMF-211	AF
VMF-218	AH
VMF(N)-533 (Night Fighting Squadron)	AI

(Below) An overall Glossy Sea Blue Noorduyn JA-1 unloading from MOUNT OLYMPUS (GC-8) during US Navy Antarctic Expedition of 1946-47 under the direction of RAdm Richard E Byrd. (Clay Jansson)

J2F-6 Duck seaplane, attached to the US Coast Guard icebreaker NORTHWIND during Antarctic OPERATION HIGH JUMP of 1946-47. Aircraft is painted overall Aluminum varnish with a Flat Black anti-glare panel forward of the windscreen. Coast Guard insignia is carried on the forward section of fuselage just above bottom wing leading edge. (USCG)

An overall natural metal finish is unusual on this Naval Air Transport Service (NATS) SBD-5 Dauntless in 1946. The NATS insignia is on the forward section of the fuselage. (William T Larkins)

SECOND MARINE AIRCRAFT WING

HEDRON MAW-2	B	HEDRON MAG 22	BK
HEDRON MAG 11	BA	VMF-113	BL
HEDRON MAG 14	BB	VMF-314	BM
VMF-122	BC	VMO-1	BR
VMF-212	BD	HEDRON MAG 53	BS
VMF-222	BE	VMF-531	BT
HEDRON MAG 21	BF	VMF-532	BU
VMR-252	BH	VMP-354	BV
VMR-952	BI		

AIRCRAFT FLEET MARINE FORCE PACIFIC

HEDRON AIR FMF PAC	P
HEDRON MAG 15	PA
VMR-352	PB
VMR-953	PC
VMF-322	PD

MARINE AIR WEST COAST

HEDRON MAR AIR WEST	W	HEDRON MAG 32	WI
HEDRON MAG 12	WA	VMF-224	WK
HEDRON MAG 25	WB	VMF-311	WL
VMR-152	WC	HEDRON MAG 33	WM
VMR-253	WD	VMF-223	WP
HEDRON MAG 31	WE	VMF-312	WR
VMR(N)-534	WF	VMF-323	WS
VMF(N)-542	WH	VMP-254	WT

AIRCRAFT FLEET MARINE FORCE ATLANTIC

MARINE CORPS AIR BASES CHERRY POINT, NC	E
MARINE CORPS SCHOOLS QUANTICO, VA	EA

ASSIGNMENT LIST OF LETTER SYMBOLS FOR MISCELLANEOUS SQUADRONS

VX-1	XA	VU-2 (ex-VJ-2)	UB
VX-2	XB	VU-3 (ex-VJ-3)	UC
VX-3	XC	VU-4 (ex-VJ-4)	UD
VX-4	XD	VU-5 (ex-VJ-15)	UE
VRU-1 (ex-VRJ-1)	RA	VU-6 (ex-VJ-11)	UF
VRU-2 (ex-VRJ-2)	RB	VU-7 (ex-VJ-7)	UH
VRU-3 (ex-VRJ-3)	RC	VU-8 (ex-VJ-8)	UI
VRU-4 (ex-VRJ-4)	RD	VU-9 (ex-VJ-9)	UK
VU-1 (ex-VJ-1)	UA	VU-10 (ex-VJ-16)	UL

NIGHT DEV RON (PAC)
(Night Development Squadron)

VCN-1	PA

NIGHT DEV RON (Atlantic)

VCN-2	LA

RESERVE AIRCRAFT

ACL No 156-46 also stated that Reserve aircraft would carry the letter/numeral system for identification as used by Training Command aircraft. The first of two letters designated the base or station, the second identified the squadron and/or class designation. Thus the markings UF would identify NAS ST Louis, Missouri U with the F signifying a fighter squadron.

The directive also called for a wide Orange stripe to be applied around the fuselage ahead of the empennage as an identification marking for Reserve aircraft.

Five weeks after the issuance of **ACL 156-46**, the office of the Chief of Naval Operations issued **ACL No 165-46**. This 12 December 1946 document directed the following changes:

Add		*Delete*
VO-3C	CI	NIGHT DEV RON (Pacific)
OP DEV RON (Operational Development Squadron)	CK	NIGHT DEV RON (Atlantic)

Carrier Aircraft Groups and Marine Fighting Squadrons were assigned the following identifying letters:

CVBG-1	M	CVG-13	P
CVBG-3	F	CVG-15	B
CVBG-5	C	CVG-17	R
CVG-1	T	CVG-19	A
CVG-3	K	CVG-21	RI
CVG-5	S	CVLG-1	SA
CVG-7	L	CVEG-1	BS
CVG-9	PS	CVEG-2	SL
CVG-11	V		

Six additional Marine squadrons were added. They were:

VMF-114	SB	VMF-513	SR
VMF-461	PA	VMF-452	MI
VMF-214	RE		

1st Marine Air Wing OY-1 on duty in Northern China, 1946. Top surface of this OY-1 is Olive Drab over Light Gull Gray undersides. The 1st Marine Division insignia, a Blue diamond with a Red number 1 in the center surrounded with White stars which represent the Southern Cross constellation, under which the Solomon Islands fighting took place. (USMC)

Lockheed P2V-1, "The 'Truculent' Turtle", flew from Perth, Australia to Columbus, Ohio in 55 hours and 17 minutes, breaking the world's record for distance without refueling with a flight of 11,235.600 miles. "The Turtle" was painted overall Glossy Sea Blue. Record flight took place from 29 September to 1 October 1946. (Lockheed)

With the issuing of **Specification SR-2f** on 2 January 1947, several changes relative to the external markings of USN aircraft came into play. External color schemes remained basically the same as they had been since the end of World War II. However, in **SR-2f**, all external color schemes were listed under one table for easy reference.

Fighter	Glossy Sea Blue
Attack	Glossy Sea Blue
Patrol	Glossy Sea Blue
Observation	Glossy Sea Blue
Marine Observation	Land Camouflage (see text)
Transport (Landplanes)	Aluminum Color
Transport (Seaplanes)	Glossy Sea Blue
Utility (Landplanes)	Aluminum Color
Utility (Seaplanes)	Glossy Sea Blue
Target Towing	See SR-2e Amendment 3 5/6/46
Training (Primary, Landplanes)	Glossy Orange-Yellow
Training (Primary, Seaplanes)	Glossy Orange-Yellow
Training (Advanced, landplanes)	Aluminum Color
Training (Advanced, Seaplanes)	Glossy Sea Blue
Rotary Wing (Observation)	Glossy Sea Blue
Rotary Wing (Training)	Glossy Sea Blue
Rotary Wing (Transport)	Glossy Sea Blue
Rotary Wing (Utility)	Glossy Sea Blue
Pilotless (Anti-Aircraft)	Per Contract
Pilotless (Anti-Ship)	Per Contract
Pilotless (Anti-Ground)	Per Contract
Pilotless (Utility)	Per Contract
Pilotless (Target Drone)	Glossy Insignia Red

In regard to the Pilotless Target Drone scheme of overall Glossy Insignia Red, it should be noted that models that were normally controlled from ground stations were to have the top surfaces of their wings painted Glossy Insignia White. The overall Red scheme concerned only drones controlled from piloted aircraft.

Because of the glossy finish applied to USN aircraft at the time **SR-2f** was issued, the use of anti-glare panels was authorized. On Glossy Sea Blue planes, the anti-glare panel, located directly forward of the pilot's windshield, was painted Non-Specular Sea Blue. On Aluminum aircraft, Non-Specular Medium Green was employed. Anti-glare panels were applied earlier, if not officially, as a practical measure.

Marine Corps observation airplanes were to be painted in the basic land camouflage color scheme, the breakdown of which was:

1). All horizontal airfoil surfaces viewed from above were to be finished in camouflage Olive Drab (ANA - 613).
2). All horizontal airfoil surfaces viewed from below were to be finished in camouflage Light Gull Gray (ANA - 620).
3). The Olive Drab of the upper surfaces of the horizontal airfoils were to be carried around the leading edge and extended back on the bottom surface approximately five percent of the wing chord and blended into the Light Gull Gray.
4). Vertical surfaces, fin and rudder, were painted Olive Drab.
5). The curved surfaces of the fuselage between the Olive Drab of the upper surfaces and the Light Gull Gray of the lower surfaces were to be blended over the intervening area in such a manner that there was a gradual color transition without noticeable demarcation between the colors.
6). Retractable landing gear were to be finished to match adjacent surfaces when retracted.

Of interest in **SR-2f** is the listing of the basic camouflage scheme, the WWII tri-color scheme, and the anti-submarine low visibility scheme from WWII. Though listed, these schemes were not authorized for use.

SR-2f brought about changes in the location of Bureau Number (BuNo), branch of service, and model designation lettering. The branch of service marking, NAVY or MARINES was to be located on both sides of the fuselage, centered with respect to a vertical line drawn from the extreme forward point of the horizonatal stabilizer to the lowest point of the fuselage and centered midway between these points.

The model designation was spaced vertically, one inch above the Branch of Service marking on both sides of the fuselage. Both of these markings were applied in 1 inch letters and numerals.

The Bureau Number (BuNo) of the airplane was to be applied vertically one 1 inch below the Branch of Service marking on both sides of the fuselage. This marking was applied in 2 inch figures.

Directions for the proper positioning of tail and wing letters were also contained in **SR-2f**. Letters applied to the aircraft's tail surfaces were to be applied to both sides of the vertical fin and rudder above the horizontal stabilizer, centered on vertical empennage surfaces.

The tail letters were 36 inches high for single letters and 30 inches high for double letters. The width of the individual strokes was to be 4 inches. In the case of double letter application where the letters may not fit within the shape of the tail at the directed 30 inch size, they may be reduced in size in order to fit.

Unit identification letters applied to the wings of naval aircraft also followed the 36 inch for single letters and 30 inch for double letters instructions. Wing letters were to be applied to the upper surface of the starboard wing and lower surface of the port wing. They were to be applied 6 inches in from the tip, and placed so as to balance the appearance of the national insignia on the opposite wing.

Individual aircraft numbers were applied on both sides of the fuselage 9 inches forward of the national insignia. On patrol planes, where the national insignia was located on the bow, the numbers were to be placed aft of the trailing edge of the wing. The top of the numerals were to be six inches below the line of the cockpit rim or cockpit rim extended.

Individual airplane numbers were also applied to the uppersurface of the right wing and lower surface of the left wing, 18 inches inboard of the unit identification letter or letters. Fuselage numbers were to be no smaller than 16 inches high and could be 20 - 24 - 28 - 32 or 36 inches at their maximum, provided they did not exceed fifty percent of the height of the projection of the fuselage side at the point of application.

Wing numerals were to be 24 inches high.

Nose and landing gear fairing numerals could be applied, if desired, in 6 inch figures.

Individual squadron insignia could also be applied on both sides of the fuselage 6 inches below the line of the cockpit rim or cockpit rim extended, directly below the most forward point of the junction of the windshield with the fuselage. The insignia could not exceed 6 inches square.

Decorations and campaign ribbons could be applied to naval aircraft if so desired. These ribbons were to be 6 inches long and 2 inches high. They were to be applied 2 inches below the squadron insignia and were to be arranged individually from top to bottom in the same order as prescribed for the wearing of ribbons by personnel. These ribbons were to be spaced vertically 1 inch apart. The ribbons could be painted on if decals were not available from the Aviation Supply Office.

(Above) Goodyear NFG-1D Corsair (92088) from NAS St Louis, Missouri. Squadron is VF-55E, "E" for escort carrier air group. In late 1946 Reserve aircraft were assigned an identifying marking to be applied to their aircraft in the form of an International Orange band. Basic color of the Corsair is Glossy Sea Blue. (USN via Jim Sullivan)

(Above) Martin PBM-3S Mariner (ex-USN PBM-3C, S666) flying out of the US Coast Guard Station in San Francisco, California in 1946. Overall Insignia White with Orange Yellow wing tips, floats, fuselage band and underside hull numbers outlined in Black. The rectangle on the side of the PBM is also Orange Yellow outlined in Black. (USCG via William T Larkins)

(Below) Coast Guard PBY-5A Catalina from San Francisco in 1946. This PBY still carries the World War II tri-color paint scheme with wing tips, floats, fuselage band and underside hull numbers in Orange Yellow outlined in Black. The letter "F" following "FRISCO" is believed to be an individual aircraft ID letter as the letter "D" is on the Mariner. At this time it is not known if the letters A, B, C, E, etc., were used on other San Francisco USCG aircraft. 552F, 552D identified both San Francisco and the aircraft. (USCG via William T Larkins)

(Below) Excellent example of the "TEST" marking applied to a Douglas BTD-1 aircraft in 1946. Overall color is Glossy Sea Blue. (NACA via Harry Gann)

POST WORLD WAR II RESERVE AIRCRAFT

Reserve aircraft were identical to Fleet aircraft in regard to their basic color and marking application. In 1947, with the issuing of **SR-2f**, a standard marking for Reserve aircraft was put into effect.

A Glossy International Orange stripe **(ANA-508)** was applied around the fuselage forward of the empennage. The width of this band was equal to the outside diameter of the blue border surrounding the circumscribed circle of the fuselage national insignia. The centerline of this band was to pass through the center of the insignia star and the band was to just meet, but not overlap the insignia border.

When the border of the national insignia was omitted, as on overall Glossy Sea Blue or Black aircraft, the Orange band terminated at the outside radius specified for such border, as if the border had been applied.

Where the fuselage insignia was located forward of the wing, as in the case of the hulls of patrol seaplanes, a 35 inch Orange band was applied aft of the unit aircraft numeral, approximately midway between the trailing edge of the wing and the leading edge of the horizontal stabilizer.

Instrument flying training aircraft still carried the fore and aft Light Green stripes on the wings and fuselage, but at this point in time, the practice of applying these stripes was at the discretion of the Commanding Officer of the station to which the airplanes were assigned.

Hospital aircraft carried the Geneva Red Cross on a Glossy Insignia White disc which was located in the spaces allotted to the unit ID letter on the wing and tail surfaces of the aircraft. The hospital insignia consisted of five Insignia Red squares arranged in the form of a symmetrical cross centered inside an Insignia White circumscribed circle. The length of the Red cross was 30 inches and the diameter of the circumscribed circle 38 inches. In cases where the 38 inch hospital insignia could not be applied due to space limitations, the insignia could be modified to best conform to the area available. However, the dimensional ratios were to be maintained.

AMENDMENT ONE to SR-2F

This amendment, with an effective date of 28 February 1947, specified that the name of the air station or the abbreviation of the unit's title could be applied to the wing and tail surfaces of aircraft in place of the unit identifying letter symbols when they were assigned.

On the vertical tail surfaces, the size of the letters used for applying this marking could be reduced to fit the area to which it was applied. If the unit name contained more than one word, it could be applied using two lines.

On the wings, the size of the letters used were to be the largest of the following series: 6, 9, 12, 15 or 18 inch. If the name of the unit or station contained more than one word, this name was to be applied in one line.

When the last three digits of the airplane's Bureau Number were used for visual identification, these numbers were to be the same size as, and placed in the locations specified for, the unit aircraft numeral.

Amendment One modified the location of the unit identifying letter. The change was not actually that noticeable, but it did occur. As before, the location of the letter/s remained on the top surface of the starboard wing and the bottom surface of the left wing. However, the center of this marking was to be placed at a distance from the wing tip equal to one-third of the distance from the fuselage to the wing tip and in a similar location to the national aircraft insignia on the opposite wing. Previously, these letter/s were applied in these locations 6 inches in from the wing tip.

The hospital insignia was also modified in **Amendment One**. The insignia continued to be the White circle with a Red cross, however, the diameter of the circumscribed circle of the hospital insignia as applied to the vertical tail surfaces was to be 2/3 of the mean chord of the fin and rudder. The Red cross was to be 15/19 of the diameter of the circumscribed circle. On the wings, the hospital insignia circumscribed circle was to be the same size as the circumscribed circle of the national aircraft insignia of the opposite wing.

Douglas R5D-2 (56541) displays Naval Air Transport Service (NATS) lettering above cabin windows with NATS lettering on top of the starboard wing. The NATS insignia appears on the nose immediately aft of the BuNo. The transport carries a natural metal finish with Non-Specular Medium Green anti-glare panel and is seen during a flight over San Francisco, California, in late 1946. (USN via Jerry Kispaugh)

A Coast Guard Sikorsky HNS-1 returns to the icebreaker NORTHWIND after an observation flight during OPERATION HIGHJUMP in early 1947. All rotary wing aircraft, at this time, were to be painted Glossy Sea Blue. However, the color of this particular HNS-1 is believed to be Non-Specular Olive Drab. (USCG via William T Larkins)

Boeing PB-1G (Flying Fortress) showing underwing lettering, overall natural metal finish and Glossy Orange Yellow wing tips and fuselage band. The lifeboat could be dropped to assist those found adrift in the open sea. (USCG via William T Larkins)

Wearing the "C" of Battle Carrier Air Group 5 (CVBG-5), an SB2C-5 of VA-6B makes a heavy landing aboard USS VALLEY FORGE (CV-45) on 18 February 1947. Piloted by Lt (JG) Otto Kuehn, Helldiver is overall Glossy Sea Blue, "C419" is Insignia White. (USN via Stan Kalas)

AMENDMENT TWO - SR-2F of 15 May 1947

At this time, planes of the Naval Air Transport Service (NATS), were authorized to carry the NATS insignia on both sides of the fuselage below the lower rim of the cockpit windows directly below the most forward point of the junction of the windshield with the fuselage. Also at this time, Marine transport aircraft attached to USMC transport squadrons were authorized to carry a gold rectangle 66 inches x 12 inches, with a 1/2 inch black border, bearing the lettering U.S. MARINES in eight inch scarlet letters. This marking was to be located in a horizontal position on the vertical fin and below the unit identifying letter/s. Marine aircraft (transport) were also authorized to carry the Marine Corps insignia on both sides of the fuselage below the lower rim of the cockpit windows directly below the most forward point of the junction of the windshield with the fuselage.

All Marine aircraft were authorized to carry the Marine Corps insignia on both sides of the fuselage, in lieu of any individual squadron insignia, provided it was placed in the same location and was the same size as specified for the individual squadron insignia, 6 inches or smaller. Both Marine Corps insignia and individual squadron insignia could not be used at the same time.

NEW NATIONAL INSIGNIA

APPENDIX I, dated 15 May 1947, featured a set of fine markings drawings and also introduced the new addition to the US national aircraft insignia. An Insignia Red horizontal bar, 1/6 the radius of the national insignia circumscribed circle, was placed in the middle of the Insignia White rectangles of the national insignia. This marked the return of the color Red to the US national insignia after an absence of some four years.

A few months after the addition of the horizontal Red bar to the national insignia the air forces of the United States received **Army-Navy Aeronautical Specification AN-I-9c**, which covered the requirements governing the size and location of the national insignia on the exterior of military aircraft. In brief, the maximum size of the national insignia as applied to wing surfaces was to be 50 inches with a minimum size of 30 inches excluding the border. Standard sizes were to have Blue circle diameters in multiples of 5 inches. The Blue circle diameter selected was to have been the standard size closest to, but not exceeding seventy-five percent of the distance between the leading edge of the wing and the aileron cut out at the point of application.

The wing insignia was to be placed at a distance from the wing tip equal to one third of the distance from the fuselage to the wing tip and tangent to the aileron cut out measured from the center of the insignia. The national insignia could be moved inboard the minimum distance necessary where wing tip floats of seaplanes interfered, or when space was not available for the minimum specified size.

Fuselage insignia size called out in the 14 August 1947 specification directed the maximum size to be 50 inches, with a minimum of 20 inches. Once again, as in the case of the wing insignia, the multiple of 5 inches rule applied, and the diameter selected was to be the standard size which came closest to, but not exceeding seventy-five of the height of the projection of the fuselage side at the point of application.

The fuselage insignia was directed to be placed on each side of the fuselage, approximately midway between the trailing edge of the wing and the leading edge of the horizontal stabilizer, but in no case could any part of the insignia be located closer than 35 inches to the trailing edge of the wing. The insignia could, however, be moved forward or to the rear of the midpoint to avoid covering transparent material. On patrol seaplanes, the insignia was directed to be placed on each side of the bow in such a position as to be completely visible when the plane was water-borne in normal load conditions. The fuselage insignia could extend over doors and emergency exits, but could not be extended over windows or such openings used during combat which would change the insignia pattern.

Experimental and Development Squadron 3 (VX-3) F4U-4 illustrates revised US national insignia brought into use by order of SR-2f Appendix I dated 15 May 1947. The XC tail letters were assigned to VX-3 in the 7 November 1946 Aviation Circular Letter No. 156-46. F4U is painted overall Glossy Sea Blue. (USN via Harry Gann)

Grumman F5F-5N Hellcat of Escort Carrier Air Group 1 catches a wire aboard USS BADOENG STRAIT (CVE-116) during 1947. (USN via Harry Gann)

Blue Angels Blue and Gold on the line in 1948. The Grumman F8F-1 Bearcat served the US Navy flight team from 1946 to July of 1949. The team first flew the Grumman F6F-5 Hellcat from April to August of 1946. (John W Caler)

Blue Angel's No 3 F8F-1 on the taxi way during a 1948 air show. Lettering and numeral 3 is Orange Yellow while Bearcat overall color is "Blue Angel's Blue" (currently FS 15080). (John W Caler)

SR-2F AMENDMENT THREE -1 May 1948

New items called out in this third amendment to **SR-2f** were that exterior color (Glossy Sea Blue) was not a requirement on experimental aircraft except on seaplanes. This did not apply to production models used for experimentation.

Branch of service markings and model designation lettering previously applied to USN/USMC aircraft in 1 inch lettering, was directed to be increased in size to 2 inches, while the airplane Bureau Number stencil was increased from 2 inches to 4 inches.

Color identification relative to squadrons made its appearance in this directive. Propeller spinners and the top 7 inches of the aircraft's fin and rudder, on both sides were to be painted to designate each squadron within the parent air group. The colors were:

1st squadron or unit - Insignia Red
2nd squadron or unit - Insignia White
3rd squadron or unit - Light Blue
4th squadron or unit - Light Yellow
5th squadron or unit - Light Green
6th squadron or unit - Black, outlined with a White border

At this time, special mention was made regarding the color scheme for helicopter rotor blades. The main rotor was to be painted overall Glossy Sea Blue with each blade tip (from tip to two inches from the tip) being painted with it's own distinctive identification stripe. The three colors assigned were:

Insignia White
Insignia Red
Light Green

In addition, Glossy Orange-Yellow warning stripes were to be painted inboard thereof on both sides, and extending from the tip.

This amendment also authorized the words US NAVAL RESERVE to be applied in 54 inch letters on both sides of non-rigid airships where the words US NAVY would normally appear. The same marking was directed for free balloons assigned to the Naval Air Reserve.

The arresting hooks (tail hooks) were to be painted with alternating Black and White 4 inch bands for maximum visibility. This practice had long been followed, being confirmed in this amendment nonetheless.

SR-15E AMENDMENT THREE - 15 June 1948

A special baked enamel paint, **AN-E-3**, was directed for application over two coats of zinc chromate primer on the hulls of seaplanes. This special coating was to extend up the fuselage side to a line 6 inches above the full load water line, and was to be faired into the lacquer coating used on the remainder of the airplane's fuselage.

A baked enamel coating for magnesium wheels was also called out. The color was to be Aircraft Gray over zinc chromate.

AN-I-9C AMENDMENT TWO -25 June 1948

Made the maximum diameter for wing national insignia 60 inches, where it had previously been 50 inches.

(Above) Number four Blue Angel F8F-1 showing application of U.S. NAVY on the underside of the port wing in Orange Yellow. Underside of starboard wing carried no markings. (John W Caler)

(Above) Douglas AD-1 Skyraider of VA-2B in 1948. Letter "M" was assigned to USS MIDWAY CVB-41 and CVBG-1 at this time. Large Insignia White fuselage numbers were common during this period. VA-2B became VA-25 in September of 1948 then VA-65 in July of 1959. (John W Caler)

(Right) Consolidated OY-1 of the USCG displaying overall Aluminum paint with Orange Yellow wing tips and fuselage band with Black outlines and underwing USCG lettering. 25 October 1948. (William T Larkins)

Marine Corps tail codes were ordered underlined in ACL 156-46 to identify USMC aircraft. This VMF-122 McDonnell FH-1 Phantom originally carried the tail letters "BC", but later in August of 1948, the squadron was reassigned the "LC" code. (USMC via Rowland P Gill)

AVIATION CIRCULAR LETTER NO.69-48 - 4 August 1948

Instructions for the updating of the visual identification system in use at this time were issued. In addition to the assignment of tail and wing letters, this letter also outlined various side items relative to the marking of US Navy aircraft.

Individual aircraft within each squadron were to be numbered consecutively as follows:

VC	- CAG Division	0- 99
VF	- Squadron	101- 199
VF	- Squadron	201- 299
VF	- Squadron	301- 399
VA	- Squadron	401- 499
VA	- Squadron	501- 599

Combat squadrons, other than Carrier Air Groups, including Patrol, Utility, Development, Observation Fleet Training and Helicopter were to be numbered with one or two digit numerals starting with the numeral 1.

The underlining of Marine Corps aircraft tail and wing letters was discontinued at this time.

Transport squadrons, Navy and Marine, were to carry the last three digits of the airplane's Bureau Number for individual aircraft identification numbering.

Reserve aircraft continued to wear the Glossy International Orange band around the fuselage.

Training squadrons within the Naval Air Training Command numbered their aircraft within each squadron with one, two, or three digit numerals, running consecutively.

Administrative and post student training aircraft attached to units other than those mentioned previously, excepting Marine Headquarters Squadrons, carried the station's name or unit name on their wings and tail; NORFOLK, FASRON 7, etc. Individual aircraft identification numbers for these units were in the form of the last three digits of the aircraft's Bureau Number.

The new listing of tail and wing unit identification letters as outlined in **ACL No. 69-48** were to be positioned on the aircraft in accordance with instructions issued in **SR-2f** of 2 January 1947. (A slight modification regarding the position of the unit identification letter as applied to the wings of USN aircraft was called out in **Amendment One to SR-2f** dated 28 February 1947.) The 4 August 1948 identification list was as follows:

CARRIER AIR GROUPS AND SQUADRONS

CVG-1 (CVG-1)	T	CVG-17 (CVG-17)	R
CVG-2 (CVBG-1)	M	CVG-19 (CVG-19)	B
CVG-3 (CVG-3)	K	VC-4	NA*
CVG-4 (CVBG-3)	F	VC-5	NB*
CVG-5 (CVG-5)	S	VC-11 (VAW-1)	ND*
CVG-6 (CVBG-5)	C	VC-12 (VAW-2)	NE*
CVG-7 (CVG-7)	L	VC-21 (CVEG-1)	BS
CVG-8	E**	VC-22 (CVEG-2)	SL
CVG-9 (CVG-9)	D* (PS)	VC-23 (CVEG-3)	MI
CVG-11 (CVG-11)	V	FAWTUPAC (VCN-1)	PA
CVG-13 (CVG-13)	P	FAWTULANT (VCN-2)	LA
CVG-15 (CVG-15)	A		

**New Assignment*
***Commissioned Sept 1948*

(Below) "Able Mabel" grabs a wire aboard USS KEARSARGE (CV-33) during carrier qualification trials in 1948. Martin AM-1 Mauler shows extreme aft positioning of Carrier Air Group 17 "R" tail code. Squadron is VA-174. The unusually small size of individual aircraft number is carried on the fuselage side. (USN via William T Larkins)

(Above) Piesecki HRP-1 carries the overall Aluminum varnish paint scheme during rescue demonstration at Elizabeth City, NC in 1949. (USCG via B R Jackson)

(Below) Douglas AD-4 Skyraider (123773) of VA-25 circa 1949. Plane has top portion of fin and rudder painted Light Green to indicate 5th squadron or unit. The seldom seen Brown Panther, VA-25 squadron insignia, is visible directly below the cockpit. "C" on the tail was the code letter assigned to CVG-6. The "E" below the windscreen indicates outstanding performance in dive bombing, rocketry and glide bombing as shown by small letters "DB, R and GB" adjacent to the "E". Pilot is Lt (jg) Matt Musick. (William T Larkins)

F8F-1 Bearcat of the 'Fighting 12A' on the flight deck of USS VALLEY FORGE (CV-45) in May of 1948. Unusual application of the Insignia White fuselage band just aft of cockpit canopy was for instant differentiation between the first and second fighter squadrons onboard at the time. VF-11A did not have a fuselage band. (USN)

NAS Atlanta, Georgia F6F-5 Hellcat from Escort Carrier Air Group 66 during summer deployment in Miami, Florida in June of 1948. Tail code "BF" indicates "B" for Atlanta, "F" for fighter, and the International Orange fuselage band indicates Reserve. (USN)

F8F-2 Bearcat onboard USS MIDWAY CVB-41 in mid-1949. Letter "E" was assigned to Carrier Air Group 8 when commissioned on 15 September 1948. CVG-8 was short lived, being decommissioned on 29 November 1949. Tip of vertical fin and rudder is painted Insignia White to designate the second squadron. (USN)

PATROL SQUADRONS

VPML, etc. designations reverted to former designation, (VP, etc.) September 1948.

VP-1	(VPML-1)	CD* (AD)	VP-29	(VPHL-12)	DE
VP-2	(VPML-2)	SB	VP-32	(VPAM-2)	DB
VP-3	(VPML-3)	CB	VP-33	(VPAM-3)	EB
VP-4	(VPML-4)	SC	VP-34	(VPAM-4)	EC
VP-5	(VPML-5)	MC	VP-40	(VPMS-10)	CA
VP-6	(VPML-6)	BE	VP-41	(VPMS-11)	MA* (AA)
VP-7	(VPML-7)	HE	VP-42	(VPMS-2)	SA
VP-8	(VPML-8)	HD	VP-43	(VPMS-3)	BG
VP-20	(VPHL-10)	DD	VP-44	(VPMS-4)	CC
VP-21	(VPHL-11)	HC	VP-45	(VPMS-5)	EE
VP-22	(VPHL-2)	CE* (AE)	VP-46	(VPMS-6)	BD* (AD)
VP-23	(VPHL-3)	EH	VP-47	(VPMS-7)	BA
VP-24	(VPHL-4)	HA	VP-48	(VPMS-8)	MB
VP-25	(VPHL-13)	BB	VP-49	(VPMS-9)	EA
VP-26	(VPHL-6)	HB	VP-51	(VPW-1)	EW
VP-27	(VPHL-7)	DC	VP-61	(VPP-1)	SD
VP-28	(VPHL-8)	CF* (AF)	VP-62	(VPP-2)	EF

TRANSPORT, UTILITY AND MISCELLANEOUS SQUADRONS

VR-1		RP*	VU-4		UD
VR-2		RA*	VU-5		UE
VR-3		RT*	VU-7		UH
VR-5		RS*	VU-9		UK
VR-6		RU*	VU-10		UL
VR-8		RH*	VX-1		XA
VR-21	(VRU-1)	RZ*	VX-2		XB
VR-22	(VRU-2)	RB*	VX-3	(CVLG-1)	XC* (SA)
VR-23	(VRU-3)	RC*	VX-4		XD
VR-24	(VRU-4)	RD*	HU-1		UP*
VR-31	(VRF-1)	RE	HU-2		UR
VR-32	(VRF-2)	RF	FAETULANT		FA
VR-44	(VR-4)	RM	FAETUPAC		FP
VO-1		UB* (CB)	ZP-1 (Lighter than air)		ZW
VO-2		UC* (CI)	ZP-2 (Lighter than air)		ZL
VU-1		UA			

MARINE CORPS SQUADRONS

AIRFMFLANT	LZ* (L)	VMF-311	WL
AIRFMPAC	WZ* (P)	VMF-312	WR
AIRFMFWESPAC	LW* (W)	VMF-322	AD* (PD)
HEDRON-1	AZ* (A)	VMF-323	WS
HEDRON-2	LL	VMF-452	AB* (BA)
HEDRON-11	LM* (LA)	VMF-461	LP* (PA)
HEDRON-12	WA	VMF (N)-114	LK
HEDRON-14	LN* (LB)	VMF (N)-513	WF
HEDRON-15	AV* (PA)	VMF (N)-531	LT
HEDRON-24	AW* (AD)	VMF (N)-533	AI
HEDRON-33	WM	VMF (N)-542	WH
MTACS-1	LI	VMP-254	WT
MTACS-2	WV* (WE)	VMP-VMP-354	LV
VMF-115	AE	VMO-1	LR
VMF-122	LC	VMO-3	AA
VMF-211	AF	VMO-6	WB
VMF-212	LD	VMR-152	WC
VMF-214	WE* (RE)	VMR-153	AC
VMF-218	AH	VMR-252	LH
VMF-222	LE	VMR-352	LB* (PB)
VMF-223	WP	VMT-1	LF
VMF-224	WK	VMT-2	WD
VMF-225	WI* (SI)		

**New Assignment*

Marine Corps stunt flying team, the Marine Phantoms, led by Lt Col Marion Carl, in flight over Fort El Morro, San Juan, Puerto Rico in 1948. Other members of the team included Capt Dan Johnson, Lt Walt Domina, Lt Vince Marzelo, Lt Louis Iglehart and Lt Fred Connelly. Co-author Doll witnessed their fine show at the St Louis Air Age Exhibition at Lambert Field in late 1948. Aircraft are McDonnell FH-1 Phantoms; squadron is VMF-122; trim color is Insignia White. (USMC via Rowland P Gill)

General Motors TBM-3U Avenger (69329) of VU-4, circa 1948, is painted in the target-tow/utility aircraft scheme for single engined aircraft. This scheme was adopted by order of Amendment 4 to Specification SR-2e of 6 May 1946. Glossy Sea Blue fuselage, Orange Yellow wings, horizontal stabilizer and vertical fin with Insignia Red wing bands and rudder. (USN via William T Larkins)

(Above) Lockheed PV-2 Harpoon from NAS Memphis, Tennessee, USNR. "M" for Memphis, "P" for patrol. Circa 1948. (John W Caler)

(Below) Goodyear FG-1D Corsair from NAS Oakland, California. "F" for Oakland; "F" for fighter. (William T Larkins)

FG-1D Corsair (V-92286) from NAS St Louis, Missouri, 1948. International Orange fuselage band indicates Reserve, "U" for St Louis, "F" for fighter. In April 1948, St Louis had four fighter squadrons, VF-54E, VF-55E, VF-75A and VF-76A. (USN via Jim Sullivan)

SR-2G 1 February 1949

This painting document was basically the same as **SR-2f**, the document issued on 2 January 1947. Basic color schemes remained the same as originally outlined in **SR-2f**, with only minor changes being called out.

SR-2g states that the last four digits of an airplane's Bureau Number may be used for individual number identification in order to differentiate it from another aircraft having the same last three BuNo digits. This applied only to non-tactical aircraft.

The marking US NAVY, 30 inches in height, was now to be applied to the top starboard and bottom port wing surfaces of all USN experimental aircraft in similar locations to the national insignia on the opposite wing.

Fuselage and floatplane propeller warning stripes were now directed to have the word PROPELLER superimposed on the Insignia Red stripe in Glossy Insignia White letters, 2 inches high. The words DANGER DANGER were to be applied perpendicular to, and centered with, respect to the word PROPELLER, one sign on each side thereof, with the arrow pointing toward the stripe. Both the arrows and lettering of DANGER were to be applied in heights and lengths of 2 inches.

Propeller warning stripes (prop tips) were to be applied as follows:

Camouflage or NS Orange-Yellow 4 inch stripe on rear face and Glossy Orange-Yellow four inch stripe on front face.

Propellers with a diameter of fifteen feet or greater used stripes measuring 6 inches from tip rearward.

Engine cowling interiors were now to be painted NS Interior Green. NS Black was previously used in this area.

ANA BULLETIN NO. 157C - 10 June 1949

This list announced yet another listing of the standard colors for Air Force and Navy aircraft. The Bureau of Aeronautics color, Light Blue became Azure Blue (ANA-609). Likewise, the Bureau's Light Green was superseded by Medium Green (ANA-612).

On the same day, 10 June 1949, a standard listing of the glossy colors used by the Air Force and the Navy appeared in **ANA Bulletin No. 166b**.

SR-2G AMENDMENT ONE - 12 MAY 1950

With the introduction of this amendment, the words NAVY and MARINES were once again applied to the fuselages of US naval aircraft after an absence of nine years. This branch of service marking was applied to the rear fuselage just forward of the empennage. The letters used were to be the largest possible accommodated on the aircraft with the selection of a standard size for the letters from the following sizes: 12, 16, 20, 24 and 28 inches.

The squadron designation, VF, VMF, etc., was also directed for application to the aircraft's fuselage at this time. This marking was to be placed directly under the branch of service marking in letters exactly 1/2 the size of the branch of service marking.

Reserve aircraft markings came under **Amendment One** also. The branch of service marking, NAVY or MARINES was to be applied to the fuselage

(Below) NAS Glenview, Illinois based F8F-1 of VF-721, 1950. Reserve squadrons were assigned single tail letters in 1950. (Eric Lundahl)

Glenview PBY-6A Catalina, 1950 (Eric Lundahl)

(Below) NAS Los Alamitos, California based Lockheed NPV-2 Harpoon of VP-772. The "L" was for Los Alamitos. (Harry Gann)

VP-23 (ex-VPHL-3) PB4Y-2 Privateers. "EH" tail letters were assigned by ACL No. 69-48 of 4 August 1948. The fuselage propeller warning stripe was directed by Specification SR-2g of 1 February 1949. (USN via Harry Gann)

NAS Grosse Ile, Michigan FG-1D Corsair. (Eric Lundahl)

(Below) NAS Minneapolis, Minnesota Beech SNB-2 (51204) in land transport overall Aluminum scheme. Aircraft type designator and branch of service are seen above the serial number. Anti-glare panel is Medium Green (Eric Lundahl)

just forward of the airplane's tail surfaces. This branch of service marking, and the name of the city to which the unit belonged were placed within the Glossy International Orange fuselage band carried by all USN Reserve aircraft. The city name was placed directly below the word NAVY or MARINES and was to be 1/2 the size of the branch of service lettering.

The branch of service marking was also applied to the undersurface of the port wing as far outboard as possible. Letters of 24 or 30 inches in height were directed for this marking (all USN combatant type aircraft).

The unit aircraft number was to be moved inboard on the undersurface of the port wing, consistent with symmetry, and reduced in size to 16 inch lettering. Unit identification letters were to be transferred to the undersurface of the starboard wing, located between the national insignia and the fuselage, 16 inches in size.

Station and support aircraft were ordered to transfer their unit or station name from the bottom port wing to the bottom starboard wing. The national insignia could be moved outboard as far as necessary to accommodate the station or unit name. This too was to be 16 inches in size. Two lines could be used for the name if needed.

All identification information, except the national insignia was to be applied to the underwing surface so that it could be read from left to right when standing in front of, and facing the aircraft.

USN - USMC TRANSPORT AIRCRAFT - BRANCH OF SERVICE MARKING

The branch of service marking for this class of aircraft was to be located, consistent with symmetry, along both sides of the fuselage, or along the outboard side of each main boom, as appropriate. In the case of low wing transports, the marking was to be located centrally above the window. For high wing transports, the marking was to be located on the fuselage either under the wing or aft of the trailing edge of the wing or along the centerline of the boom. The marking was to be as follows:

For US Navy and US Navy Reserve aircraft - UNITED STATES NAVY.
For US Marine Corps and Marine Corps Reserve aircraft - UNITED STATES MARINES
For aircraft operated jointly by the US Navy and US Marine Corps or by Reserve components - UNITED STATES NAVY

The squadron designation or station name was to be located below the branch of service marking on all USN/USMC transport aircraft. The lettering used for this marking was to be 1/2 the size of that used for the branch of service marking. If the station or squadron marking could not be located underneath the branch of service marking then it could be placed aft along the fuselage, below the centerline.

On transport aircraft assigned to the Reserve, in cases where the branch of service marking was placed along the fuselage above the windows, the station name was to be placed along the centerline of both sides of the rear fuselage, just forward of the empennage. This was in addition to the station letter on both sides of the vertical fin and rudder. If the International Orange band used to identify Naval Reserve aircraft interfered, the continuity of the band could be interrupted to permit the station name to be applied to the fuselage. Again, the station name lettering was to be 1/2 the size of the lettering used to spell out the branch of service name.

Marking instructions regarding the wings of transport aircraft were the same as all other models previously mentioned.

If the station name was applied to the fin and rudder, it was not to be applied to the fuselage.

Douglas R4D-5 during early 1950. Eight of these were acquired by the Coast Guard between May of 1943 and July of 1944. Aircraft is overall Aluminum varnish with an Orange Yellow fuselage band outlined in Black. The branch of service marking is carried above the windows as ordered in SR-2G Amendment One. (USCG)

Overall Glossy Sea Blue VS-23 TBM-3 Avengers in flight over USS CHARR SS-328 in early 1950. All letters and numbers are in Insignia White. (USN)

F4U-4s formerly of VMF-218 (AH) sit on Guam awaiting shipment back to the United States. Planes were being returned to the US as part of the Fleet Marine Force, Guam, re-deployment took place in January of 1950. (USMC)

KOREAN WAR

F4U-4B Corsair of VF-53 on USS VALLEY FORGE (CV-45) in mid-1950. Air Group 5 was the first naval unit to carry out a strike on North Korea. Tip of the rudder and fin above CVG-5 "S" is Light Blue for 3rd squadron. (USN)

ADDITIONAL TAIL LETTERS

On 25 June 1950, the Republic of South Korea was invaded by forces from North Korea. Naval Aviation went to war on 3 July when Air Group 5 from the USS VALLEY FORGE (CV-45), attacked an area in and around Pyongyang, northwest of Seoul. This was the first of many missions for the men and machines of US Naval Aviation during the Korean War.

As Naval aviation units quickly expanded to meet the Korean crisis the need for additional unit markings was obvious. On 29 July 1950, **Aviation Circular Letter No. 43-50** was issued. This letter added thirteen new tail letter assignments to the new squadrons formed since the advent of the Korean War.

The new assignments were:

VC-3	NP	VS-22	SL
VC-6	NF	VS-23	MI
VC-33	SS	VS-24	SI
VC-35	NR	VS-25	SK
VC-61	PP	VS-31	SP
VC-62	PL	VS-32	SR
VS-21	BS		

Additional tail letter assignments for new Marine Corps squadrons also came into existence during the Korean War. From data on file in the Marine Corps Historical Branch, courtesy of Major John Elliott, USMC (Ret), the following is presented:

VMC-1	RM	HMR-162	HS
VMJ-1	MW	HMR-163	HP
VMO-2	LS	VMA-251	AL
MAMS-12	WA	MAMS-33	WM
MAMS-16	WW	VMF-314	LW
VMA-121	AK	VMA-332	MR
HMR-161	HR		

RESERVES INTO ACTION - KOREA 1950-51

Almost immediately following the United States' entry into the conflict in Korea, the Naval Reserve was called into action. Fourteen squadrons were activated during July of 1950. Seven more were activated in September of that year and in February of 1951, an additional thirteen were called to active service. By the first anniversary of the North Korean invasion, eight more reserve squadrons had been activated, bringing the total number of squadrons called up during the first year of the conflict to forty-two.

Reserve squadrons called into action that first year were:

DALLAS	VA-702, FASRON 701
ANACOSTIA	VP-661
AKRON	VF-653
ATLANTA	VF-671
COLUMBUS	FASRON 691
GLENVIEW	VF-721, VA-728
GROSSE ILE	VP-731
JACKSONVILLE	VF-742, VP-741
LOS ALAMITOS	VF-781, VF-783, VP-772
MEMPHIS	VF-791, VP-FAS 795
MINNEAPOLIS	VP-812
NEW ORLEANS	VF-821, FASRON 821
NIAGRA FALLS	VA-859
NEW YORK	VF-831, VF-837, VS-831
MIAMI	VS-801
OLATHE	VF-884, VP-FAS 885
OAKLAND	VF-871, VF-874, VP-871, VS-871
SEATTLE	VP, FASRON 895, VP-892, VS-892
SQUANTUM	VP, FASRON 915, VF-916, VS-913
ST LOUIS	VA-923, VF-921
DENVER	VF-713
NORFOLK	VP-861
WILLOW GROVE	VP-931, VS-931

VF-113 F4U-4 from USS PHILIPPINE SEA (CV-47), 1950. Fin and rudder tips are Light Blue. Aircraft is overall Glossy Sea Blue with Insignia White lettering. (USN)

When the reserve aircraft went into action with the regular Navy, the Glossy International Orange band and the station tail letters were removed and replaced with the tail code being used by the air group to which the reserve unit was attached. However the unit often kept its reserve squadron designation on their aircraft even though the tail letter change was effected.

RESERVE TAIL LETTERS - 1950

The following tail letters were assigned to Naval Air Reserve units circa 1950:

DALLAS	D	NEW YORK	R
ANACOSTIA	A	MIAMI	H
AKRON	L	OLATHE	K
COLUMBUS	C	OAKLAND	F
GLENVIEW	V	SEATTLE	T
GROSSE ILE	I	SQUANTUM	Z
JACKSONVILLE	F	ST LOUIS	U
LOS ALAMITOS	L	DENVER	P
MEMPHIS	M	NORFOLK	S
MINNEAPOLIS	E	WILLOW GROVE	W
NEW ORLEANS	X	BIRMINGHAM	T
NIAGRA FALLS	H		

CARRIER AIR TASK GROUPS - KOREA

Air Task Groups (ATG) were non-commissioned units formed with squadrons transferred from regular Carrier Air Groups. They existed for approximately eight years, from early in the Korcan War to early 1959. Their formation was the result of two factors, one being combat experience in Korea which showed that Air Groups as then constituted with five squadrons (three or four VF and one or two VA squadrons) could not be operated effectively aboard existing carriers; the other being a Congressional limitation on the number of Air Groups in the aeronautical organization.

Withdrawal of one squadron from each of the existing Air Groups corrected operational difficulties and also provided spare units, permitting the

Cdr John "Tex" O'Neill's F4U-4 Corsair serves as backdrop for Phil Sea deck hands in 1950. VF-113 squadron insignia and name "Little Lady" can be seen near the windscreen. Cdr O'Neill's name also appears on fuselage just forward of the VF-113 insignia. (USN)

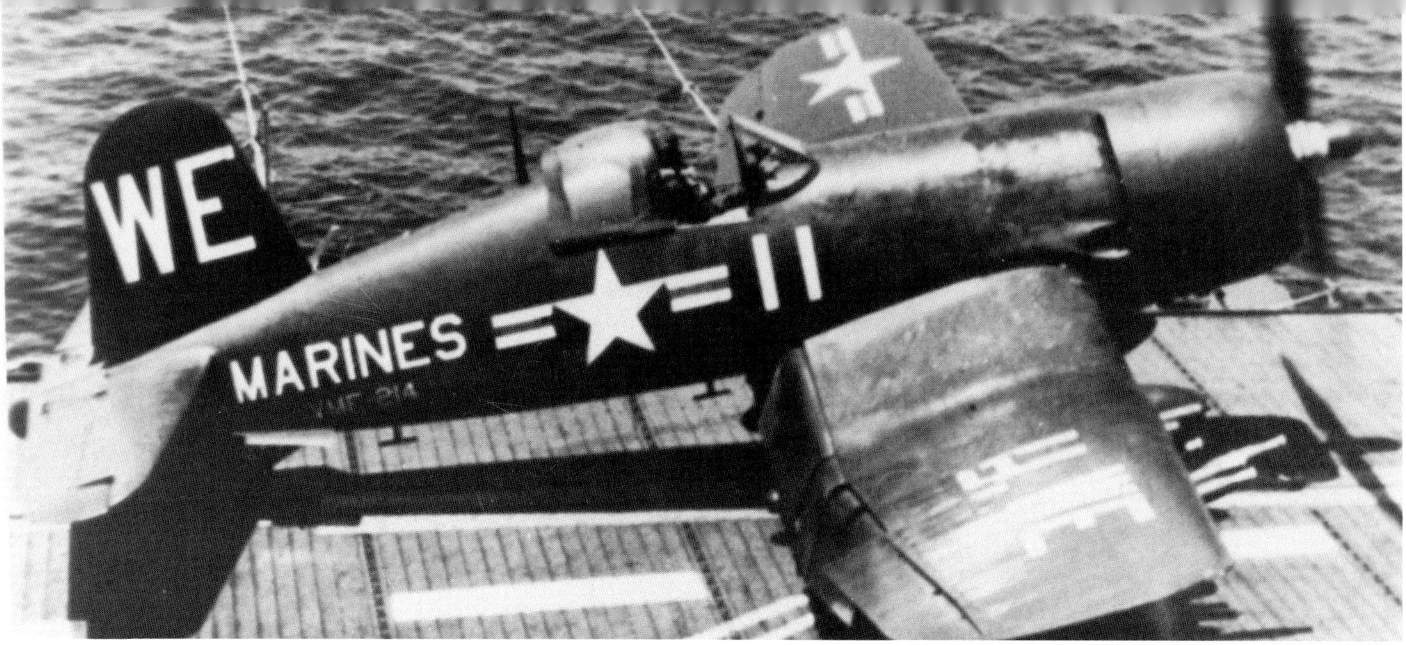

F4U-4B Corsair of VMF-214 about to launch from USS SICILY (CVE-118) in 1950. Operating from Sicily on 3 August 1950, VMF-214 became the first unit of the First Marine Aircraft Wing to engage in combat operations in Korea when they carried out a rocket and bombing attack on Chinju. Squadron designation and branch of service lettering was ordered applied to USN/USMC aircraft by SR-2g of 12 May 1950. (USMC)

formation of Air Task Groups. Because ATGs were non-commissioned and held a title implying formation of a special unit to meet specific needs, and therefore of a temporary existence, Congressional limitations were, in theory, not violated.

The fact that ATGs were non-commissioned and also non-official, put them in the *ghost* unit category and created a number of administrative problems regarding assignment of staff, accounting for personnel, and delivery of mail. It also meant that they were not listed in the Naval Aeronautic Organization, or in any tabulations which show unit assignment and allowances, and until June of 1955, were even omitted from tabulations of Fleet unit locations. A complete accounting of them is now difficult.

From data available in Aviation History and Unit files, eight ATGs existed from 1951 to early 1959. Of these, two served in the Korean War and were in existence longer than any of the others. The peak of eight ATGs was reached in 1955, and maintained into 1958. The following is what is known of the existence of each.

ATG-1 Established in October of 1951. Began service in Korea in December of 1951; disestablished 23 February 1959.

ATG-2 In existence in June of 1952. Began service in Korea in July 1952; disestablished on 1 April 1958 (but was listed in Fleet Locations Lists into January of 1959.

ATG-3, ATG-4, ATG-181, ATG-182, ATG-201, ATG-202 formed after mid-1953 and will be discussed later.

SR-2H — 16 JUNE 1952

The final full scope painting directive issued during the Korean Conflict was **SR-2h**. **SR-2h** was nearly the same as **SR-2g** of 1 February 1949. However certain new requirements were introduced in **SR-2h** and the following is a run-down on those orders.

The words US NAVY and the aircraft Bureau Number shall be applied to both sides of the vertical stabilizer on naval aircraft (transport) operating with the Military Air Transport Service.

An addition to the propeller warning marking as applied to aircraft fuselages and floats was directed in **SR-2h**. The word DANGER and the accompanying arrows were to be superimposed on a stripe of Glossy Insignia White, 3 inches in width. The height of the letter and arrow remained at 2 inches.

A helicopter tail boom warning marking was ordered for helicopters having tail rotor blades which revolve in a vertical plane. A Glossy Orange-Yellow band, encircling the tail boom for a distance of approximately 33 inches just forward of the plane rotation of the blade was applied. Centrally superimposed on this band was an Insignia Red arrow of appropriate size, with the arrow pointing toward the rotor blade. Above the arrow, the word DANGER was to be applied, and below the arrow, the words KEEP AWAY. These words were applied using Black paint, and were approximately 2 inches in height.

(Below) Grumman F9F-2 Panther of VMF-115 in flight in 1950. Second Marine Aircraft Wing, MCAS Cherry Point, North Carolina. (USMC)

(Above) VMFN-531 F7F-3N Tigercat on a flight over the east Coast of United States in 1950. (USMC)

(Below) Headquarters Squadron One, First Marine Air Wing, in Korea, acquired a Douglas R4D-5 during 1950. It is finished in the overall Aluminum scheme for landplanes with Black lettering. Insignia Red propeller warning stripe is applied just aft of co-pilot's window. (USMC)

Grumman F9F-2B Panthers of VMF-311 at Tonpo in December of 1950. Color is overall Glossy Sea Blue with an Insignia Red trim color on the tips of the vertical tail surfaces. (USMC)

(Below) F4U-5 Corsair of VMF-212 on Tonpo Airfield, Korea, on 10 November 1950. The unit was redesignated VMA-212 by the end of the Korean War. (USMC)

(Above) VMO-6 observation planes on Tonpo Airfield near Hungnam, Korea on 6 November 1950. Nearest plane is a Consolidated-Vultee TN-OY-2 and is painted overall Glossy Sea Blue. The other planes are believed to be OY-2s and are painted in the USMC land camouflage scheme, Olive Drab top surfaces over Light Gull Gray undersides. The "TN" designation was applied to training aircraft. (USMC via Rowland P Gill)

(Left) Six Advanced Training Unit 4 F6F-5 Hellcats in flight on 18 December 1950. (USN via W T Larkins)

Tail rotor blades were to be finished in Glossy Orange-Yellow from the rotor tip to 6 inches from the tip on both sides of the blades, followed by a 6 inch wide Non-Specular Black stripe on both sides of the blades, followed by a 6 inch wide Glossy Orange-Yellow stripe on both sides of the blade.

Aircraft having wing-tip tanks with fins installed in such a manner that the fins extended outboard in a horizontal plane, and which fins are such a distance from the ground that personnel may walk into them inadvertently, were directed to apply warning markings. These markings consisted of a Glossy Orange-Yellow band encircling the fin from the tip to a distance 2 inches inboard from the tip, followed by a Glossy Insignia Red band encircling the fin from a distance 2 inches inboard from he tip to a distance 4 inches inboard from the tip.

Naval Attache (ALUSNA) aircraft carried the words UNITED STATES NAVAL ATTACHE TO (NAME OF COUNTRY) on both sides of the fuselage located just under the pilot's cockpit. For the benefit of foreign personnel, the same lettering as used above, but worded in the language of the country to which the Attache was accredited was directed to a placed approximately 2 inches below the American inscription. On aircraft such as the R4D or larger, the American inscription was to be located above the centerline of the fuselage with the foreign inscription located below the centerline of the fuselage. Also the lettering used on R4D or larger aircraft was to be 4 inches in height. For smaller aircraft, the lettering was reduced proportionately.

The American flag was to be applied on the underside of the left wing approximately under the aircraft national insignia, as it appeared on the top side of the wing. The flag was to be centered symmetrically and applied so that an observer on the ground, with the airplane approaching, would view the flag with the blue field forward and to his left, and with the stripes extending outboard. The flag was to be in the proportions of 1.0 feet in width and 1.9 feet in length, in accordance with standard American flag requirements. In no case, however, was the width to exceed seventy-five percent of the distance between the leading edge of the wing and the aileron cut-out at the point of application. In all cases, the largest size flag which could be accommodated on the wing was to be used.

The flag was also applied to the tail surfaces of all ALUSNA aircraft. The flag was to be painted on both sides on single tailed aircraft, and for aircraft having multiple vertical tail surfaces, the flag was to be applied only on the two outboard sides. The flag on the left side of the aircraft was applied with the blue field forward and the stripes extending aft. The flag on the right side of the aircraft was applied with the blue field forward and the stripes extending aft. The flag on the right side of the aircraft was to be applied with the blue field aft and the stripes extended forward. The flag was to be centered symmetrically on the surface.

For R4D and larger aircraft, the flag was to be 3.0 feet in width by 5.7 feet in length. On smaller aircraft, the length of the flag was not to exceed seventy-five percent of the chord at one-half the height of the vertical surface

from the horizontal surface. On aircraft with twin vertical surfaces (stabilizers), the length of the flag was not to exceed seventy-five percent of the chord at one-half the height of the vertical surfaces.

Basic color schemes of USN/USMC aircraft stayed as before with the application of all markings, unit ID, numbers, etc., also being the same as before. Individual squadron embellishments appeared throughout the Korean War years, 1950-53, and continued until the 1955 major color scheme change from overall Glossy Sea Blue to NS Light Gull Gray and Insignia White.

The dimensions of the various colorful squadron designs are, of course, unknown since these markings were under no official directive governing their color or measurements and were usually the brainchild of crewchiefs and pilots.

On 1 July 1953, just twenty days before the ending of the Korean War, a new listing of tail letter assignments was posted. From the Schedule of Aeronautical Organization, the following list of then current tail letter assignments is given.

CVG-1	T	VC-9	FG
CVG-2	M	VC-11	ND
CVG-3	K	VC-12	NE
CVG-4	F	VC-33	SS
CVG-5	S	VC-35	NR
CVG-6	C	VC-61	PP
CVG-7	L	VC-62	PL
CVG-8	E	VS-20	SV
CVG-9	N	VS-21	BS
CVG-10	P	VS-22	SL
CVG-11	V	VS-23	MI
CVG-12	D	VS-24	SI
CVG-14	A	VS-25	SK
CVG-15	H	VS-26	SH
CVG-17	R	VS-27	SM
CVG-19	B	VS-31	SP
VC-3	NP	VS-32	SR
VC-4	NA	VS-38	ST
VC-5	NB	VS-30	SW
VC-6	NF	VS-36	SD
VC-7	NH	VS-37	SU
VC-8	NC	VS-39	SN

SR-202 - 1 AUGUST 1953

SR-202, a short ten page painting directive issued in mid-1953 brought about two major painting changes relative to the operation of USN aircraft. The most radical of these changes was the adoption of a high visibility color scheme for multi-engined training aircraft. Single engined trainers retained the overall Glossy Orange-Yellow scheme.

"Quick and dirty" should be the title of this Korean War US Marine Corps photograph. VMF-323 F4U-4B Corsair (63025) illustrates the results of an on-the-spot tail letter change. Marines in background are helping to position another VMF-323 Corsair prior to a mission. (USMC via Rowland P Gill)

Marine Training Squadron One (VMT-1) F4U-4 Corsair from MCAS Cherry Point, North Carolina during 1951. This colorful Corsair features Light Green fuselage, cowl and wing stripes to indicate an instrument trainer. These stripes, outlined with Insignia White, were applied at the discretion of the Commanding Officer of the station to which the aircraft was assigned; per SR-2f (1947). ('d E C Darby)

(Below) Lockheed TO-2 from Naval Test Center, Patuxent River, Maryland on 13 April 1951. Fuselage national insignia is not applied according to specification; tips of White star should not touch outer edge of Blue circle. Overall natural metal with Black lettering. (USN via W T Larkins)

F9F-2B Panther of VF-721 from NAS Glenview, Illinois Reserve unit in flight over Korea in 1951. Squadron was activated for Korea on 20 July 1950 and went aboard USS BOXER (CV-21) in March of 1951. Nose trim is Insignia Red for first squadron. Leading edges of wing are natural metal. (USN via B R Jackson)

"Yvonne III" a VF-791 F4U-4 over Wonsan, Korea in July of 1951. This Memphis Reserve unit was activated for Korean War duty on 20 July 1950 and went aboard USS BOXER (CV-21) on 27 March 1951. The tail is tipped with Insignia White for second squadron. (USN via Jerry Kishpaugh)

(Below) Composite Squadron 4 (VC-4) F4U-5N noses over during landing accident on board USS LEYTE (CV-32) on 3 November 1951. Pilot is Ensign L H Resek. Aircraft BuNo is 124691. (USN via Jim Sullivan)

The high visibility, or *Hi-Viz* scheme, consisted of two colors, Glossy International Orange and Glossy Insignia White. Instructions for painting this scheme, using the Beech SNB "Bugsmasher" as an example as follows:

> The colors applied to the fuselage terminate two inches below the passenger windows and extend aft to about the middle of the hatch; they then terminate on a line extending aft to the bottom of the horizontal stabilizer fairing. The colors applied to the wings terminate along the centerline.

SOLAR HEAT REFLECTION SCHEME

SR-202 directed that all medium and heavy transport aircraft were to receive the Solar Heat Reflection Scheme. Other types of transport and utility aircraft could also be painted in the heat reflecting scheme, at the discretion of the local CO, provided they predominately operated in areas of high temperature.

Using an R6D as the example, the solar heat reflecting scheme was as follows:

> The upper surface of the fuselage was to be Glossy Insignia White beginning at the top forward edge of the pilot's enclosure and extending aft, splitting each side of the vertical stabilizer and fading out in the vicinity of the tail cone and extending down on each side to the bottom row of windows. The horizontal stabilizer and the major portion of the vertical stabilizer was to remain aluminum color.

ANTI-GLARE PANELS

On all pilot-operated aircraft, Non-Specular paint of the same or approximately the same color was to be substituted for glossy paint on all surfaces which would produce glare in the pilot's or co-pilot's eyes. Anti-glare areas were to be painted NS Medium Green on Aluminum colored aircraft, Glossy Orange-Yellow trainers, and Glossy International Orange and Insignia White Trainers.

RADOMES - RADIO ANTENNA HOUSINGS

The color of assemblies fabricated of resin impregnated glass fabric, radomes, radio antenna housings, noses, fairings, wing tips and intake ducts, for which rain erosion protective finishes were required, were to be in the natural black of the applied protective finish. This finish was, and is, a rubber-like material which was and still is applied in many coatings until the proper thickness is achieved.

SR-202 directed a color scheme change for non-rigid airships. The envelope (gas bag) remained Aluminum color, but the control car was to be painted Glossy Sea Blue. All other markings remained the same. This change was also called out for free balloons.

F2H-2 Banshee (123259) at MCAS Cherry Point, North Carolina carries tail letters assigned in August 1948 and branch of service and squadron markings ordered in May 1950. VMR-252 Curtiss R5C-1s (C-46s) are in the background. (USMC via Rowland P Gill)

Nineteen fifty three soon became just another year, and with it, the passing of the forty-second year of United States Naval Aviation. The developments during those forty-two years would astound even the most progressive thinkers. Along with the brilliant mechanical and scientific progress accomplished by US Naval Aviation, we have seen how important the seemingly un-important field of color and markings turned out to be. Color had come full circle, from purposes of concealment to technical coatings for anti-corrosion, back to concealment, even in the highly advanced 1960s, 1970s and into the 1980s.

In 1953, the United States managed to cool a hot war in Korea, and America again prepared for a time of peace, although it was be an uneasy peace...

(Right) Reserve Group 102 onboard the USS BON HOMME RICHARD (CV-31) during their tour in Korean waters from 30 May to 30 November 1951. Onboard at that time were VF-781 (Los Alamitos) in F9F-2s, VF-783 (Los Alamitos) in F4U-4s, VF-874 (Oakland) in F4U-4s, and VA-923 (St Louis) in AD-2s. Also onboard was VC-3 in F4U-5Ns; VC-11 in AD-4s, and VC-35 in AD-4s. (USN)

(Below) NAS Denver based VF-713 F4U-4 over Korea. VF-713 was activated for Korean service on 1 February 1951 and went aboard USS ANTITAM (CV-36) on 15 October 1951 and rotated 5 March 1952. Insignia White trim is on vertical tail surfaces and propeller hub. LCdr R L Doering, commanding. (USN via Jim Sullivan)

(Above) F9F-2B Panther of VMF-311 at K-3 airstrip Pohang, Korea in 1952. With 445 combat missions to its credit (at the time). White 2 flew its first mission on 10 December 1950. Mission marks are Insignia White. (USMC via Rowland P Gill)

(Left) F4U-4 Corsairs of NAS Los Alamitos based Reserve fighter squadron VF-783. Squadron wore tail letter "D" while operating as part of CVG-102 during their tour in Korean waters. Tip of vertical tail surfaces are painted Insignia White for second squadron. Prop hubs also carry identifying color. (VU-7 via W T Larkins)

HEDRON One F7F-3P Tigercat in flight over Korea during May of 1952. (USMC via Rowland P Gill)

(Above) HRS-1 helicopters of HMR-161 during OPERATION ROCKET at Panjong-ni, Korea, 21 August 1952. These machines carry good examples of helo markings of the period. (USMC via Rowland P Gill)

(Right) McDonnell F2H-2P Banshee of VMJ-1 in Korea, 1953. VMJ-1 became a photo squadron in February 1952, flying 5,025 combat missions. Tip tank marking is Insignia Red outlined in White. (USMC via Rowland P Gill)

(Below) VMA-332 (MR) F4U-4B Corsairs with White bands and Red polka dots. VMA-332 replaced VMA-312 onboard USS BAIROKO (CVE-115) on 8 June 1953. Photo taken on 27 July 1953, the last day of the Korean War. (USMC via Rowland P Gill)

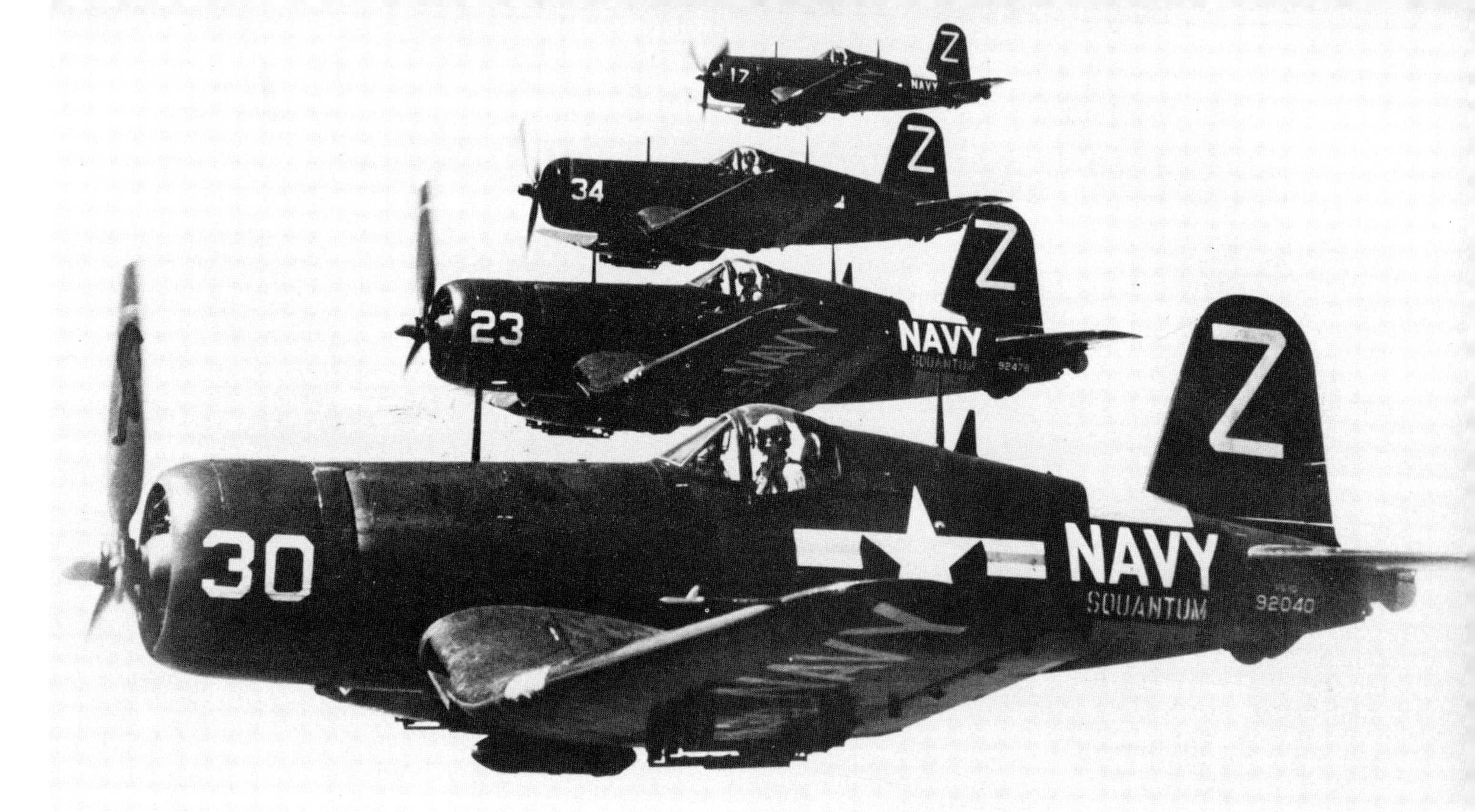

POST KOREAN WAR

NAS Squantum, Massachusetts FG-1D Corsairs of VF-916 illustrate extreme aft positioning of the Reserve fuselage band. (Eric Lundahl via Harry Gann)

The Armistice ending the Korean Conflict was signed on 27 July 1953, ending three bitter years of war. The United States Armed Forces once again returned home to peaceful shores.

Air Task Groups (ATGs) were still being formed, as mentioned previously, and in November of 1953 ATG-181 was established. But by the end of 1959, these Air Task Groups would no longer exist in the US Navy and as ghostly as they appeared they would disappear. Below is a listing of all Air Task Groups formed except for ATG-1 and ATG-2, covered earlier. ATG-3 formed in November of 1954, established in March 1955, disestablished in April of 1958.

ATG-4 Established 30 March 1955. Disestablished 19 January 1959.
ATG-181 Established in November 1953. Disestablished 15 August 1958.
ATG-182 Appears in Fleet Locations first in July 1955 and probably established in that month; no information on dissestablishment — but disappears from Fleet Locations in January of 1959.
ATG-201 Formed in 1954. Established in June of 1955. Disestablished in November of 1958. Disappears from Fleet Locations in November of 1958.
ATG-202 First appears in Fleet Locations during June of 1955. Disestablished in January of 1959.

United States Navy and Marine Corps aircraft were still under the requirements of **SR-202** and **SR-2h** with most combat aircraft retaining their Glossy Sea Blue color scheme. It would be another two years before a major change in paint schemes would appear on US Naval aircraft. The only major change occuring during these two years was the model designation change for airships. The change was made to conform with the designations for heavier-than-air aircraft. The envelope designation letters "K" and "N" were replaced by manufacturer's letters. Standard suffix numbers and letters were uniformly applied and the patrol class of airships were divided into patrol and anti-submarine classes. Thus the ZPN became the ZPB-1 and the ZP2K became the ZSG-2, G for Goodyear. This change became effective of 19 April 1954.

On 27 April 1954, the Chief of Naval Operations (CNO) approved Project 125 of the aircraft carrier improvement program, which provided for the installation of an angled deck, enclosure of the bow for improvement of seaworthiness, and many other changes that would modernize all carriers that had just been completed under Project 27A. (Project 27A had been approved in 1947 for the modification of ESSEX class carriers. Principal changes being strengthening of the flight decks, installing more powerful hydraulic catapults, increasing the elevator strength, doubling the aviation fuel storage, providing jet blast deflectors, etc.). The carriers were undergoing a major face lifting, the aircraft would soon follow suit.

VC-35 AD-3 Skyraiders in flight over San Diego, California in March of 1952, bracketing two AD-4Qs of the same unit. Application of NAVY on underside of wings is visible as are alternating bands of Black and White on tail hooks. (USN via W T Larkins)

(Above) Douglas R5D-4Z "VIP" transport with highly polished natural metal exterior. Fleet Logistic Air Wing insignia and Marine Corps Commandant's four star Scarlet and Gold placard are carried below the cockpit. Propeller tips are Insignia Red, White and Blue. Aircraft was assigned to VR-1 (RP) when this photo was taken in March 1952. (USMC via Rowland P Gill)

Example of Reserve band applied to HUP-2 helicopter based at NAS Glenview, Illinois. Band is International Orange with helicopter being painted overall Glossy Sea Blue. (Eric Lundahl via Harry Gann)

VMA-312 F4U-4B Corsair, flown by Captain Richard S Togerson, USMC, ran into trouble onboard the USS BAIROKO (CVE-115) on 11 April 1952. Insignia White squares adorn engine access cowling giving testimony to squadron's nickname, "Checkerboard Squadron". VMA-312 was redesignated from VMF to VMA on 1 March 1952. (USMC via Rowland P Gill)

Itami, Japan based VMR-253 Fairchild R4Q-1 Flying Boxcar (128736) in natural metal with UNITED STATES MARINES applied to fuselage per SR-2g, Amendment One of 12 May 1950. Numerals on nose, 736, are the last three digits of the BuNo. (USMC via Rowland P. Gill)

VMF-235 F4U-4 being off-loaded from the carrier USS CAPE EXPERANCE (CVE-88) onto NAS Ford Island, Pearl Harbor (TH). This Corsair was part of forty-four F4U Corsairs that were delivered to MCAS Kaneohe on 14 March 1952 to give the newly reactivated air station its initial aircraft. Trim colors are Light Yellow. (USMC via Rowland P Gill)

Standard Reserve markings are applied to these four VF-695 F6F-5s Hellcats from Columbus, Ohio on 12 July 1952 while the squadron was on summer training exercise at Miami, Florida. NAVY and name of city the squadron operated in was ordered on Reserve aircraft by May 1950 Amendment One to SR-2g. (USN via Jerry Kishpaugh)

VS-871 Grumman AF-2S Guardian over the Golden Gate Bridge on 14 February 1953. Oakland was one of several Reserve bases that shared letter assignments with other stations during the early 50s; NAS Jacksonville, Florida also carried the letter "F" on their Reserve aircraft. (USN via Jerry Kishpaugh)

(Below) Jacksonville, Florida Reserve AF-2S Guardian carrying the letter "F" which it shared with NAS Oakland, California. The sun and salt air has oxidized the Glossy Sea Blue to nearly a non-specular finish. (Clay Jansson)

(Below) F6F-5P Hellcats during April of 1953 from NAS Pensacola, Florida with Orange Yellow wing tips, rudder and prop hub. White "NATTCen P-19" appears on topside of starboard wing with smaller example of same lettering painted on vertical fin with station name PENSACOLA directly underneath. Overall color is Glossy Sea Blue. "NATTCen" is acronym for Naval Air Technical Training Center. (VFP-63)

(Below) Lockheed TV-2s of ATU-200 from Naval Auxiliary Air Station Kingsville, Texas in August of 1953. Medium Green anti-glare panels are carried both in front of the cockpit canopy and on the inside surfaces of the wing tip tanks were directed by SR-202 of 1 August 1953. Nose radome coating was also covered in SR-202. (USN via Jerry Kishpaugh)

Overall Glossy Sea Blue F4U-4 Corsair belonging to Commander Air Group 17 (CAG 17) LCDR Stanley 'Swede' Vejtasa. All letters and numerals are White. Summer 1946.

SB2C-5 of Air Group 75. The Helldiver is overall Glossy Sea Blue with White letters and numerals. The tail band is Insignia Red. Mid 1946.

Goodyear NFG-1D Corsair of Reserve VF-55E at NAS St Louis in overall Glossy Sea Blue with International Orange numerals, letters, and tail band on the fuselage. Letters and numerals on the tail are in White.

F8F-1B Bearcat of VF-17 in overall Glossy Sea Blue with Yellow numerals and letters in late 1946.

Natural metal Douglas SBD-6 Dauntless of the Naval Air Transport Command, San Francisco, California, 1946. (William T Larkins)

Douglas R4D-5 with newly applied solar heat reflecting Insignia White fuselage top as directed by SR-202 of 1 August 1953. Letters "AZ" are for HEDRON One, Korea. (USMC via Rowland P Gill)

(Above) General Motors built TBM-3E Avenger from the Reserve base at Akron, Ohio. Tail letter "L" was shared with NAS Los Alamitos, California. (Eric Lundahl via Harry Gann)

(Below) North American FJ-1 Fury attached to Reserve base Olathe, Kansas. The International Orange Reserve band is barely visible on the rear fuselage. (Eric Lundahl via Harry Gann)

(Below) F9F-7s Panthers of VF-21 in flight, October 1953. This squadron was awarded AirLant Battle Efficiency Pennant on 6 October 1953 for setting new records for jet equipped squadrons. LCdr G D Acker was in command at the time. Trim color is Insignia Red indicating the first squadron. (USN via Jerry Kishpaugh)

(Above) Colorful F9F-5P Panther of VMCJ-3 out of MCAS El Toro, California during 1954. Tail letters are "TN", trim colors are an Insignia Blue field with Insignia White stars outlined with a border of Insignia Red and White. Overall color of plane is Glossy Sea Blue. (USMC via Rowland P Gill)

(Above) Crewmen scramble for their Martin P5M-1G Marlin seaplane called out on a search and rescue mission at USCG station at Elizabeth City, North Carolina in January of 1954. Orange Yellow stripe around fuselage with overall Aluminum varnish paint scheme. (USCG)

(Below) USS TARAWA (CV-40) is scene of VF-102 flight deck action in March of 1954. Tip of fin and rudder on the Panthers is Insignia White. (USN via Harry Gann)

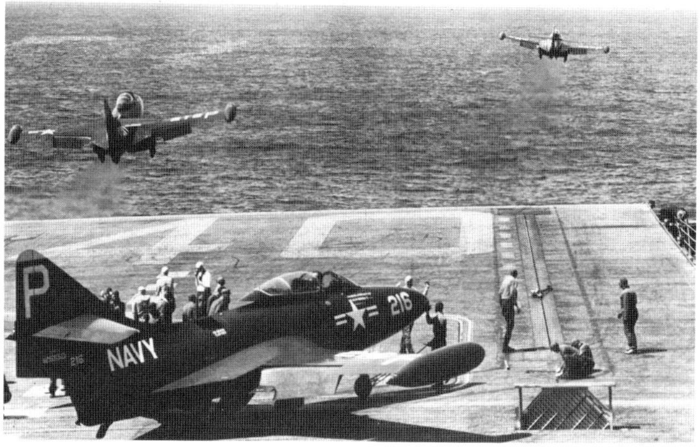

F2H-3 Banshees of VF-31 flying over Midway (CVA-41) during June of 1954. Two of the Banshees carry the experimental natural metal finish and Insignia Red trim color.

US Coast Guard PBM-3S Mariner flying out of San Francisco. It is painted overall Glossy Insignia White with Orange Yellow fuselage band. The engine cowls are Olive Drab.

Naval Air Transport Service (NATS) R5D-2 in natural metal with a Medium Green anti-glare panel, and Black letters and numbers.

F8F-1 Bearcat of VF-12A aboard VALLEY FORGE at Sidney, Australia in May of 1948. Overall Glossy Sea Blue with White letters, numbers, and fuselage band. The Red Bar was added to the national insignia as of May 1947.

Overall Glossy Sea Blue Douglas AD-2 Skyraider of VA-6B off USS Coral Sea (CVB-43), Guantanamo Bay, Cuba, February 1948. (Stan Kalas collection)

Overall Glossy Sea Blue Douglas AD-2Q Skyraider of VC-150 at San Francisco, California, 30 October 1949. Pilot is Engisn W B Whitten. (William T Larkins)

Overall Glossy Sea Blue F5F-5N Hellcat nightfighter of Escort Carrier Air Group 1 off BADOENG STRAIT (CVE-116) in 1947.

Goodyear NFG-1D of VF-76A from NAS St Louis. Overall Glossy Sea Blue, this Corsair carries White letters and numbers and the International Orange rear fuselage band of a reserve unit.

An overall Glossy Sea Blue USMC McDonald FH-1 Phantom of VMF-122. All letters and numerals are White. Marine Corps tail codes were ordered underlined in ACL156-46.

The Blue Angel's "Beetle Bomb", a Grumman F8F-1 Bearcat painted overall Glossy Orange Yellow with Blue letters, 1949. (Harry Gann)

(Above) F9F-5 Panthers of CVG-8 on the line at NAS Oceana, Virginia in 1954. Mixture of color schemes is evident. Both the Navy and Marine Corps experimented with unpainted clear coated schemes, beginning with the directive of 29 April 1952 (Aer-AE-421, Serial 08821). Unpainted schemes proved unsatisfactory in the salt air and were cancelled on 16 February 1955. Trim color on these Panthers is Light Yellow. (USN)

(Below) F7U-3 Cutlasses attached to FASRON-12 at NAS Miramar, California in February 1954. At this time the national insignia (wing) was located at 90 degrees to the centerline of the fuselage. Later, in September 1954, MIL-614OA (ASG) called for the national insignia application on swept winged aircraft to be placed in such a position on the wing that the line through the top of the star point and its center were perpendicular to the line formed by the constant fifty percent chord line of the wing which passes through the center of the star. (Arthur Schoeni)

(Above) NAS Glenview, Illinois F2H-1 Banshee carries the oversized NAVY applied to the underside port wing. Maximum size was to be 30 inches. (Eric Lundahl via Harry Gann)

(Below) CVG-12 F9F-6 Panther with colorful Insignia Red and White nose trim and Red tip of fin and rudder. The leading edge of the wings were painted aluminum. (Harry Gann)

(Above) NAS Pensacola, Florida T-28B Trojan in overall Glossy Orange Yellow as specified for single engined trainers in 1954. Medium Green anti-glare and exhaust panel, with Black lettering are carried. (USN via W T Larkins)

(Below) F9F-8 of VF-13, part of Air Task Group 201. Insignia White stars on Light Blue trim. Wing tips, bottom of nose and diagonal band across top of fuselage and wing were also Light Blue. ATG-201 was formed in 1954 but not formally established until June of 1955. The unit was dis-established in 1958. (Harry Gann)

(Above) VMA-323 in their colorful marked F9F-5 Cougars during 1954. Trim color is Light Green outlined in White. (Clay Jansson)

(Below) TN-OY-1 from the Naval Missile Range at, Point Mugu, California. Overall Glossy Sea Blue paint. (Harry Gann)

Lockheed NPV-2 Harpoon of VP-772 out of NAS Los Alamitos. Overall Glossy Sea Blue with White numbers and letters, and an International Orange Reserve Band behind the National Insignia.

Beech SNB 'Bugsmasher' out of NAS Minneapolis, Minnesota in the overall Aluminum land transport scheme. Anti-glare panel is Medium Green, numbers and letters are Black.

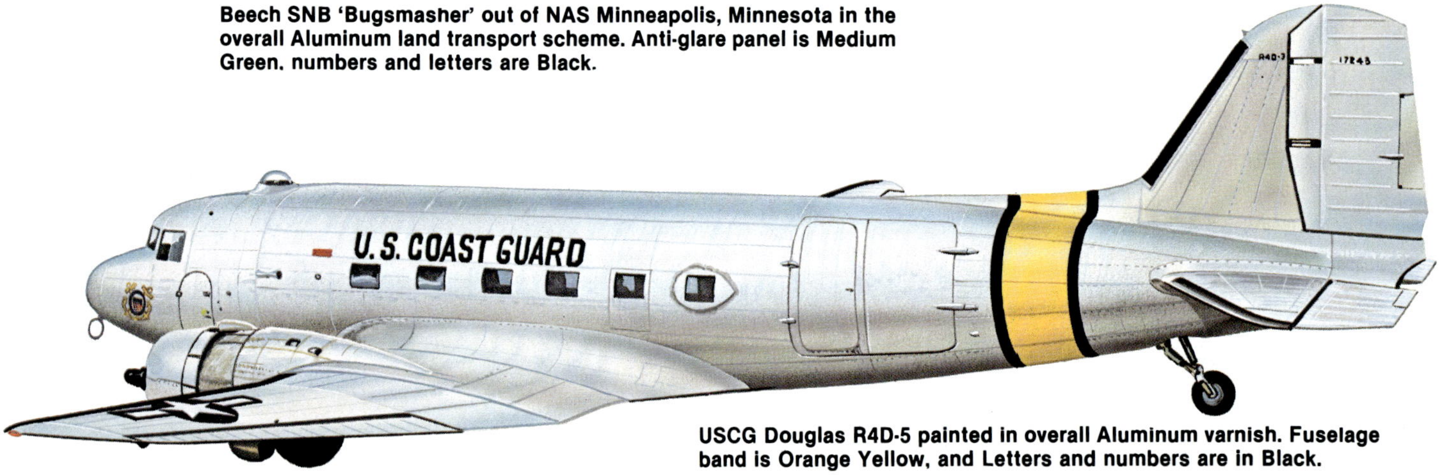

USCG Douglas R4D-5 painted in overall Aluminum varnish. Fuselage band is Orange Yellow, and Letters and numbers are in Black.

Vought F4U-5 Corsair, CAG CVG-4, MIDWAY (CVB-41) during 1950 Med Cruise. Squadron colors of Blue, Red, White, Blue and Yellow are carried on the top of the tail. (Fred Drinkwater)

Overall Glossy Sea Blue Vought F4U-4 Corsair of VMA-312 aboard BAIROKO (CVE-115) off Korea during 1952. (USMC)

F4U-4 of VMF-214 'Black Sheep' off SICILY (CVE-118), Korea, 1951. Overall Glossy Sea Blue, the numerals and letters are Insignia White as are the fifty strike markers, four tank markers and the E for Battle Efficiency. Painted in front of the E is the Squadron insignia, a Presidential Unit citation, and the Efficiency Pennant.

USMC Vultee TN-OY-2 of VMO-6 at Tonpo Airfield, Korea, 6 November 1950. Overall Sea Blue with White lettering and numerals.

USMC F7F-3P Tigercat of HEDRON ONE, Korea, May 1952. Overall Glossy Sea Blue with White Letters and numerals.

"Blue Tail Fly", F9F-5 Panther of VF-153 off PRINCETON (CV-37), May 1953. Front of 'Fly' is natural metal with Black lettering and rear portion is Glossy Sea Blue with White lettering. "Blue Tail Fly" is Light Blue.

'VICE-VERSA' of VF-111 off the PRINCETON (CV-37), successor to the "Blue Tail Fly", the front of this F9F-5 is Glossy Sea Blue and the rear is natural metal. The numerals 314 are on the nose while 15 is carried on the tail.

Douglas F3D-2 Skyknight of VF-14 leaves deck of USS INTREPID (CVA-11) on 9 November 1954. "High Hat" squadron was part of Air Task Group 201 at this time. Trim color is Light Yellow. The CVA designation replaced CV and CVB designations on 1 October 1952; the CVL designation was discontinued 15 May 1959. (The Hook VF 02053, USN Photo)

(Below) Beech JRB-4 at USCG Air Station, Elizabeth City, North Carolina, 16 January 1955 carrying the standard Coast Guard Aluminum paint scheme with a black anti-glare panel. Rudders are White. (USCG)

HO4S-2G during 1955 carries overall Orange Yellow paint scheme as directed on 18 June 1951. All rotary winged aircraft were to receive this scheme. (Harry Gann)

A NEW COLOR SCHEME

F2H-4 Banshees of VMF-214 at MCAS Kaneohe Bay. Non-specular Light Gull Gray top surfaces over Glossy Insignia White undersides was the new scheme as directed by MIL-C-18263 (Aer) 23 February 1955. (Clay Jansson)

MIL-C-18263(AER) 23 FEBRUARY 1955

On 16 February 1955, an advance letter, Aer-AE-421 was sent to all concerned parties in Naval and Marine Corps Aviation announcing the distribution of a new painting document. This document, **MIL-C-18263(Aer)**, was prepared after several years of careful study of camouflage schemes for carrier based combat aircraft. For the first time since the close of World War II, the United States Navy and Marine Corps began a complete modernization program of paint schemes for operational aircraft.

Aer-AE-421 also called for the cancellation of a previous Bureau of Aeronautics letter **Aer-AE-421, Serial 08821** of 29 April 1952. This letter had called for the evaluation of unpainted fighter aircraft for use on carriers. Apparently this was an attempt at the unification of all United States Aircraft and had proved unsatisfactory for Navy and Marine Corps aircraft due to the high rate of corrosion encountered at sea, even though Navy and Marine aircraft were provided with a clear lacquer overcoating.

Listed below are the basic color schemes as they appeared in MIL-C-18263(Aer)

Attack (VA)	NS	Light Gull Gray
	G	Insignia White
Fighter (VF)	NS	Light Gull Gray
	G	Insignia White
Marine Observation Landplanes(VO)	NS	Olive Drab
(Except helicopters)	G	Insignia White
Patrol (VP)	SG	Seaplane Gray
Transport Landplanes(VR)		Aluminum
	G	Insignia White
Transport Seaplanes (VR)	SG	Seaplane Gray
Trainer (VT) — Landplane		
Single reciprocating Engine	G	Orange Yellow
Multireciprocating Engine	G	International Orange
	G	Insignia White
Trainer (VT) — Seaplane		
Advanced	SG	Seaplane Gray
Primary	G	Orange Yellow
Trainer (VT) — Jet		
Intermediate	G	International Orange
	G	Insignia White
Primary	G	Orange Yellow
Target Towing (VU)	G	Orange Yellow
	G	Engine Gray
	G	Insignia Red
Utility (VU) — Landplanes		Aluminum
Utility (VU) — Seaplanes	SG	Seaplane Gray
Warning (VW)	SG	Seaplane Gray

NS = Non-Specular
G = Glossy
SG = Semi-Gloss

Helicopters (H)		
Cargo unloading (HC)	NS	Light Gull Gray
Observation (HO)	NS	Light Gull Gray
Transport (HR)	NS	Light Gull Gray
Submarine Search and Attack (HT)	NS	Light Gull Gray
Trainer (HT)	G	Orange Yellow
Utility (HU)	NS	Light Gull Gray
Target Drone (KD)	G	Insignia Red
Drone Control (KD)	G	Orange Yellow
	G	Insignia Red
	G	Engine Gray
Airships (ZP)		
Patrol and Escort		Aluminum — Envelope
	NS	Light Gull Gray — Car
Trainer (ZT)		Aluminum — Envelope
	NS	Light Gull Gray — Car
Free Balloon (Trainer) (ZT)		Aluminum — Envelope
	NS	Light Gull Gray — Car
Search (ZS)		Aluminum — Envelope
	NS	Light Gull Gray — Car

NOTE: Seaplane Gray and Engine Gray are the same color, the difference being Seaplane Gray is semi-gloss while Engine Gray is glossy.

F7U-3 Cutlass of VF-124 onboard HANCOCK (CVA-19) in September of 1955. The carrier Air Group 12 "D" and all lettering is Black as is the field of the tail insignia with Orange Yellow skull and crossed cutlasses. (USN)

HUP-1 of NAS Glenview in overall Glossy Sea Blue with an International Orange band, and White lettering and numbers.

Lockheed TV-2 of Advanced Training Unit 200 (ATU-200) in overall Natural Metal with Black numbers and letters. Anti-glare panels in front of windscreen and on inside of wing tanks are Medium Green.

Grumman F9F-8 Cougar of VF-13 Air Task Group 201 (ATG-201). Overall Glossy Sea Blue with Light Blue and White trim, and White letters, numerals and stars.

AD-6 Skyraider of VA-42, Air Task Group 181 during FORRESTAL's Caribbean shake down cruise, January of 1956 to 31 March 1956. Overall Glossy Sea Blue with White Numbers and letters and Glossy International Orange trim.

de Havilland UC-1 Otter of VX-4 during OPERATION DEEPFREEZE wearing the special Arctic scheme of overall Aluminum trimmed with International Orange, and Black letters and numbers.

F7U-3 Cutlass of VF-124 of Carrier Air Group 12 aboard HANCOCK (CVA-19), wearing the new Light Gull Gray over Glossy Insignia White. All lettering and numerals are Black, and the squadron insignia is Orange Yellow on a Black field.

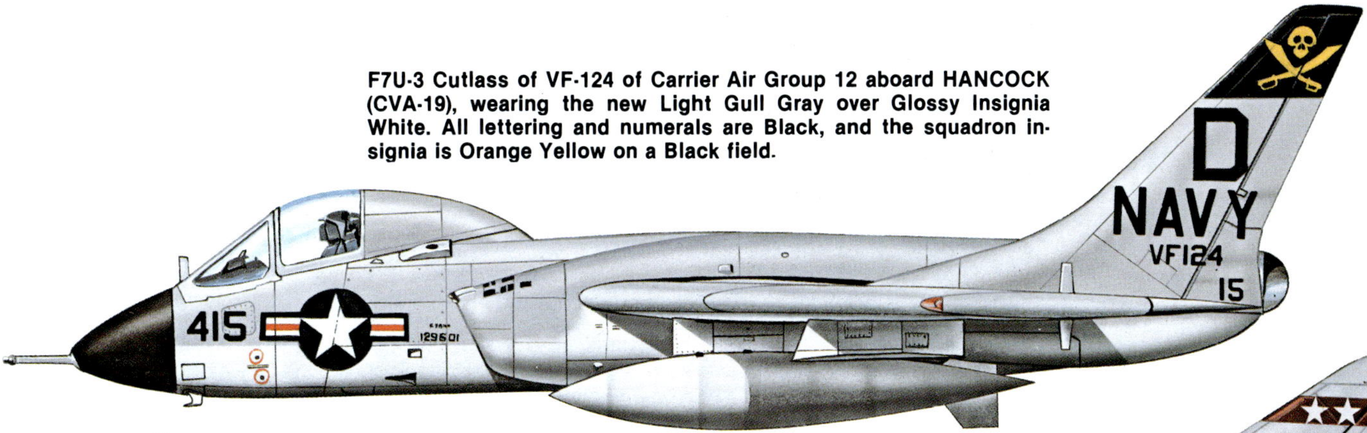

Douglas F4D-1 Skyray of VC-3 out of Moffet Field in May of 1956. Scheme is the new Light Gull Gray over Glossy Insignia White with Black lettering. Band on upper tail is Maroon with White stars.

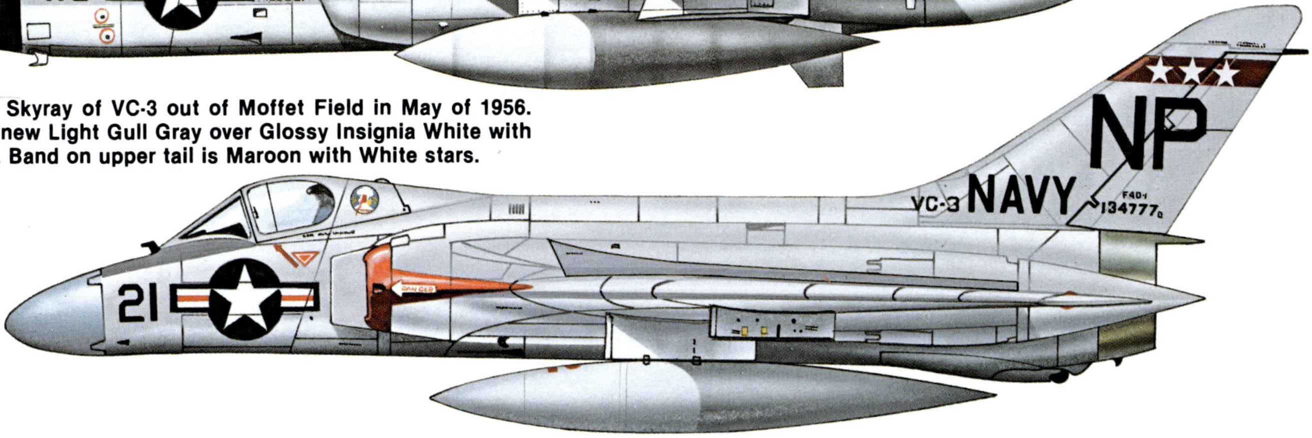

Grumman F9F-8T Cougar of VF-124 in overall Glossy Insignia White trimmed in Fluorescent Red Orange, San Francisco, California, 1960. (Harrison Rued)

Lockheed T2V-1 in overall Glossy Insignia White with Fluorescent Red Orange trim at NAS Miramar, California, in April of 1962. (Jerry Kishpaugh)

Vought F8E Crusader of VF-141 off CONSTELLATION (CVA-64), carrying the now standard USN scheme of Light Gull Gray over Glossy Insignia White, 1963. (Bude Donato)

McDonnell F3H Demon of VF-161 off ORISKANY (CVA-34), 1963. (Bude Donato)

Vought AU-1 Corsair with Lt Col John Holt, USMC, in the cockpit in March of 1956. The Light Gull Gray over Glossy Insignia White scheme was not overly common to the Corsair. The Black anti-glare panel broke up any camouflage advantage the Gray/White scheme might have provided. MCAS El Toro, California (Clay Jansson)

Under the specification **MIL-C-18263(Aer)**, all aircraft designed for carrier operations were to be painted in a Non-Specular Light Gull Gray and Glossy Insignia White color scheme.

All horizontal airfoil surfaces viewed from above were to be painted NS Light Gull Gray, while those viewed from below were to be painted Glossy Insignia White. On the edges of the horizontal airfoils, the NS Light Gull Gray of the upper surface was to be blended into the Glossy Insignia White under surface color at the mid-section; or alternatively, the NS Light Gull Gray could be carried around the edge and extend back on the lower surface approximately one inch, and blended into the Glossy Insignia White.

The leading edges of airfoils and frontal surfaces were to be painted in an approved rain-erosion resistant finish. At this time the approved finishes for metal surfaces were an aluminized color and those approved for glass fiber reinforced plastic assemblies varied from Natural Tan to Black. The erosion-resistant finish was to be applied in such a manner that it would extend from the first row of rivets or fasteners on the upper surface to the first row of rivets or fasteners on the lower surface.

All horizontal control surfaces were to be painted Glossy Insignia White, both upper and lower.

All vertical control surfaces were to be painted NS Light Gull Gray, both sides.

The fuselage section viewed from above was to be painted NS Light Gull Gray, and the surfaces viewed from below were to be painted Glossy Insignia White. The vertical surfaces or side areas were to be painted in the following manner. The NS Light Gull Gray of the top surface was to extend down to the line of maximum width of the fuselage surface and the Glossy Insignia White was to be applied to the lower portion of the fuselage. In the case of a substantially straight-sided aircraft, the colors were to join on the straight portion of the side approximately an inch above the juncture of the side and bottom surfaces.

All carrier aircraft with multi-engines were to be painted in the same color scheme. The engine nacelles were to be painted in the same manner as the fuselage procedure.

The vertical fin was to be painted NS Light Gull Gray on both sides.

All aft-facing radomes on carrier operating aircraft were to be painted Glossy Insignia White. Black or other dark colors were prohibited on the aft-facing radomes of these aircraft. Inclusive in this specification was that all belly radomes were to be painted Glossy Insignia White as well, and that this painting document would take precedence over any provision to the contrary, such as the warning note DO NOT PAINT, which appeared on many radomes.

MIL-C-18263(Aer) also related for the first time that, officially, the interior of the wheel wells of all aircraft were to be painted Glossy Insignia White.

All land based observation aircraft were to be painted in the land camouflage color scheme of NS Olive Drab and Glossy Insignia White.*

The horizontal airfoil surfaces that were viewed from above were to be painted NS Olive Drab, while those viewed from below were to be painted Glossy Insignia White. The NS Olive Drab of the upper surface was to be carried around the leading edge and extend back on the lower surfaces approximately 1 inch, and blend into the Glossy Insignia White.

All vertical surfaces, fin, rudder, etc., were to be painted NS Olive Drab.

The fuselage, viewed from above, was to be NS Olive Drab and the portion viewed from below was to be Glossy Insignia White. The NS Olive Drab of the upper surface and the Glossy Insignia White of the lower surfaces were to be blended over the side areas in such a manner that there would be a gradual color transition without a noticeable demarcation between the two colors.

The landing gear, if retractable were to be painted in such a manner that they would match the adjacent surfaces when retracted. If non-retractable, or fixed, they were to match the prescribed color of the aircraft.

The propeller spinners and wing walkways were to be painted NS Olive Drab, the same as the wing, except where an anti-skid material was used. In this case, the walkways could be NS Black per the specification for walkway material.

The land camouflage color scheme was applied mainly to Marine Corps Observation (VO) landplanes and did not include helicopters.

All patrol planes were to be painted Semi-Gloss Seaplane Gray over the entire surface of the aircraft. This paint scheme was to be used on both land based patrol aircraft and seaplane patrol aircraft.

A special patrol plane scheme was called for, but was to be used only when specifically authorized by the Bureau of Aeronautics. This paint scheme was to be Semi-Gloss Seaplane Gray on the upper surfaces and Glossy Insignia White on the lower surfaces, and was applied in the same procedure as the carrier scheme.

** In reality this pertained to OE-1 and OE-2 aircraft only. This color scheme was applied in much the same manner as the carrier scheme.*

Two VMF-115 F4D-1 Skyrays with noteworthy undersurface lettering. The "Ford" bringing-up the rear has MARINES properly applied, while the lead aircraft has the lettering reversed. Tail and wing tip stripes are Insignia Red, White and Blue. "AE" is the tail modex. (Harry Gann)

(Above) VMF-122 FJ-2 Furies in flight on 6 December 1954 in the experimental natural metal scheme that was used from April 1952 until February of 1955. A few aircraft from each squadron tested the unpainted finish which was top coated with clear lacquer. Fuselage stripes, nose intake cowl and tail markings were Light Green and White. (USMC via Rowland P Gill)

All anti-submarine warfare aircraft would employ the carrier scheme, if the aircraft was designed for carrier operations. If the aircraft was solely designed for land operations, they would incorporate the color scheme of patrol planes. All helicopters were exempt from this particular paint scheme.

All utility aircraft, landbased, remained in the aluminum finish as prescribed in **SR-202**. Utility aircraft that were used for the purpose of target towing retained the same color scheme as stated in **Amendment 4 SR-2E**, 6 May 1946, except that the Glossy Sea Blue color was replaced with Glossy Engine Gray. This same color scheme was also to be used for drone control aircraft.

(Below) More VMF-122 Furies, this time the FJ-3. The overall Glossy Sea Blue paint is highlighted by the squadron's colors as they fly over the Neuse River near Oriental, North Carolina on 3 April 1956. Date of photo would indicate that VMF-122 was some fourteen months late in effecting the Gray/White scheme directed in February of 1955. (USMC via Rowland P Gill)

VMF-122 FJ-3 on 30 July 1956 in the new paint scheme of Light Gull Gray over Glossy Insignia White. (USMC via Rowland P Gill)

Douglas TA-3B Skywarrior of VAH-123 wearing Light Gull Gray over Glossy White scheme with Fluorescent Red Orange trim. The warning trim on the engine intake is Insignia Red. 1963 (Bude Donato)

Grumman HU-16C Albatross in the Search and Rescue scheme, 1964. NAHA on the upper tail has a definite oriental flavor. (Jerry Kishpaugh)

Douglas TA-4F Skyhawk belongs to Commander Marine Aircraft Group 32 (MAG 32), 1968. Trim color on the aircraft is Black, however, the trim color on the drop tanks is Dark Blue. (Duane Kasulka)

Coast Guard HU-16D Albatross in overall Gloss Insignia White, trimmed in Coast Guard Red (No 40). The small stripe aft of the cockpit is in Coast Guard Blue (No 41). USCG 1971. (Hideki Yamauchi)

(Above) Vought DF-8F Crusader of VC-8, 1969. The fuselage is Engine Gray, the wings are Orange Yellow and the tail is International Orange. Lettering and numerals are in both Black and White. (Duane Kasulka)

(Below) Douglas A-4C Skyhawk of VA-305, USN Reserve, 1971. Trim is Dark Green and White with stylized tail letters in Black. (Harry Gann)

All aircraft used in training were to carry a special paint scheme that would aid in identification in heavy traffic areas and enhance safety in flight. In the past, some of the training aircraft were aluminum, and others carried training colors which resulted in added problems during overhaul and repair.

Under **MIL-C-18263s(Aer)**, all single reciprocating engine, primary jet and helicopter aircraft used in training were to be painted all over Glossy Orange Yellow, except for anti-glare areas. All multi-reciprocating engine and jet aircraft used in training were to be painted in Glossy International Orange and Glossy White color scheme. In the event that either of these aircraft were used by both the Training Command and Operational Commands, the aircraft would be painted in the training colors, regardless of the assignment. All combat aircraft used in training would retain their combat colors.

All utility landplanes that operated in heavy air traffic areas, and that did not carry the high visibility Glossy International Orange and Glossy White, could apply this color scheme locally when authorized by the Commander Air Force, Atlantic or Pacific Fleet; Chief of Naval Air Reserve Training; or in case of aircraft assigned to an air station, the Chief of the Bureau of Aeronautics.

A new color scheme for aircraft operating in the Arctic area was introduced in **MIL-C-18263(Aer)**. When authorized, a paint scheme of Glossy International Orange applied to all tail and fuselage surfaces measured from the extreme tail end of the airplane for a distance of thirty percent of the total length of the aircraft, and on the top and bottom surfaces of both wing tips, extending inboard from each wing tip a distance equal to fifteen percent of the wing span. The National Insignia on the fuselage and wings could not be overlapped by the Glossy International Orange, but the reverse was permitted. The insignia could not be altered in size or location with the application of this paint scheme. The balance of the aircraft was to remain in the color prescribed for the aircraft type. The main purpose for this paint scheme was to assist in the spotting of downed aircraft against a snow background. This paint scheme excluded all helicopters; however, helicopters using the Arctic color scheme were painted allover Glossy International Orange except for areas that required extensive masking. These areas remained in their basic color scheme for ease of application.

The solar heat reflection paint scheme described in **SR-202** for all medium and heavy transport planes remained unchanged in **MIL-C-18263s(Aer)**.

All warning aircraft which were designed for carrier operations were painted in the carrier aircraft color scheme of NS Light Gull Gray and Glossy Insignia White. All others were to be painted in the patrol plane color scheme of over all Seaplane Gray.

All helicopters not operating with the Arctic color scheme, were to be painted over all NS Light Gull Gray, with the exception of those used in training.

All airships, patrol and escort, trainer, free balloon and search remained in their previous Aluminum color for the envelopes, but the cars would now carry the Light Gull Gray color.

All items such as helicopter blades, engine cowlings, hubs, spinners, etc., remained the same as described previously.

Douglas F4D-1 Skyray of VC-3 at NAS Moffett Field, California, 19 May 1956. Band across tail surfaces is Glossy Maroon as directed by MIL-I-18464(Aer) of 9 March 1955 for VC squadrons. (William T Larkins)

(Above) Markings can be seen to full advantage on this Oakland Reserve F4U-4 Corsair in September of 1956. (William T Larkins)

(Below) USCG P5M-2G Marlin 'T tail' from the Coast Guard Air Station, Elizabeth City, North Carolina in October 1956. The anti-glare panel is Medium Green. (USCG)

(Above) "Green Pawns"' AD-6 Skyraiders on flight deck of FORRESTAL (CVA-59) in early 1956 during its Caribbean Shakedown Cruise. Tip of the vertical fins and rudders of VA-42 AD-6s are Glossy International Orange. That this is a period of change-over between the old and new scheme is obvious. Eight squadrons comprised Air Task Group 181 onboard CVA-59 at this time. (Douglas via Harry Gann)

(Below) VX-6's most famous aircraft, "QUE SERA SERA", the R5D-5 which landed at the South Pole on 31 October 1956. Arctic paint scheme with the solar reflecting top is carried. ('d E C Darby)

(Above) North American FJ-4 Fury of VMF-451. Insignia Blue trim with Insignia White stars on the new Standard Gray/White scheme. 23 November 1956. (VMJ-1)

(Below) Martin XP6M-1 Seamaster on 11 September 1956 carrying the special patrol plane scheme of Semi-gloss Seaplane Gray over Insignia White. This scheme was called out in MIL-C-18263(Aer) of 23 February 1955. (USN via Harry Gann)

Vertol HUP-1 from MCAS El Toro, California in overall Glossy Orange Yellow scheme in 1957. Specializing in helicopters, Piasecki changed its name to Vertol Aircraft. (Clay Jansson)

MIL-I-18464(AER) 9 MARCH 1955

On 9 March 1955, a new directive covering the markings, and the markings alone, was dispatched to all Naval and Marine Corps departments concerned. Up until this time, all markings and painting information for the Navy and Marine Crops had been carried, more or less, under a single document, such as **SR2h, SR2g**, etc. Now there would be two separate documents issued, one for markings under the code of **MIL-I-**, and one for painting under a code of **MIL-C**. These documents became known as **MIL** specs, short for **Military Specifications**.

Under **MIL-I-18464(Aer)**, dated 9 March 1955, all heavier than air aircraft were to be marked in the following manner.

The fuselage markings were to be positioned, insofar as was practical, so that all letters and numerals on the fuselage and vertical tail surfaces would be perpendicular to the fuselage reference line. All identifying information that was to be located on the under surface of the wings, except the National Aircraft Insignia, was to be applied so that it could be read from left to right when standing in front of or facing the aircraft. On swept-back wings and wings of variable sweep, all letters and numerals were to be applied symmetrically along the 50 percent constant chord line as was required for the National Insignia.

BRANCH OF SERVICE

The branch of service marking was to be applied to all aircraft, except in the case where it was known in advance that a particular aircraft was intended for use by the Marine Corps. This note was intended for the information of the manufacturer in the process of readying an aircraft for delivery to the service.

The location of the branch of service marking on the fuselage was to be on both sides of the aircraft, just forward of the empennage. The size of the lettering was to be the largest size possible that could be accommodated on the aircraft. Selection was to be from the following standard sizes: 12, 16, 20, 24, 30 and 36 inches. Location on the wings was to be on the under surface of the left wing, and as far outboard as possible on all aircraft except those intended for carrier use, and patrol aircraft which were painted White on the underside of the wing in accordance with **MIL-C-18263s(Aer)**. No branch of service unit identifying letters or numerals appeared on the underside of the wings, only the National Insignia and any small maintenance markings needed. Size was to be 24, 30 or 36 inches for the word NAVY and 12, 16, 20, 24, 30 or 36 inches for the word MARINES. Once again, size depended on the aircraft and was to be the largest possible that could be accommodated.

The branch of service for all US Navy and US Naval Reserve aircraft was to consist of the word NAVY. For all aircraft operated by the US Marine Corps and Marine Corps reserve, the word would be MARINES. All aircraft that were jointly operated by the two services, the word was to be NAVY.

(Right) AD-6 of VA-65 over Mount Fuji in November of 1958. The 'FIRST OF THE FLEET', VA-65, was flying from MIDWAY (CVA-41) at the time. Trim colors on 502 were Light Green to designate the fifth squadron. (Stan Kalas)

(Below) Grumman F9F-8B Cougar flown by Blue Angels leader Cdr Zeke Cormier in 1956. (Harry Gann)

(Above) F4D-1 Skyray attached to Fleet All Weather Training Unit, Pacific (FAWTUPAC) on 16 November 1956. Horizontal control surfaces were painted Insignia White. Light Gull Gray and Insignia White scheme applied to 'Ford' with a Medium Green anti-glare panel. (Douglas via Harry Gann)

(Above) VA-65 AD-6s in November of 1958. Placement of markings and Insignia White horizontal control surfaces can be seen. In late 1956 cockpit interior colors were tested, and by January of 1957 Dark Gull Gray began to replace Interior Green during aircraft overhauls and at the factory as new aircraft rolled off the line. (Stan Kalas)

HSS-1 helicopter of Anti-submarine Squadron 9 painted overall Light Gull Gray, February 1958. Side and bow number (Black 8) was to be as large as possible without exceeding 48 inches except when two digit numbers were used. This was according to the directive issued on 9 March 1955, covering individual ASW helicopter ID markings. (USN via Harry Gann)

(Below) Fleet Marine Force Douglas R4D-8 (rebuilt R4D-6), carrying the Solar reflecting top color and all standard markings. April 1958. (Clay Jansson)

MODEL DESIGNATION AND BUREAU NUMBERS

All operational aircraft were to carry a model designation and Bureau airplane serial number (BuNo). The Bureau Number consisted of numerals assigned to the airplane by the Bureau of Aeronautics. These BuNos were to be applied to both sides of the fuselage, and centrally located under the horizontal stabilizer. On aircraft having twin booms, such as some transports, the BuNo was to be located on the outboard side of each boom between the National Insignia and the horizontal stabilizer. In both cases the Bureau Number was to be symmetrically located two inches below the model designation. Letters and numerals of the model designation were to be 2 inches in height, and the numerals of the Bureau Number, 4 inches in height. If space permitted, the application of the full Bureau Number was placed on the vertical surface for radio call numbers. If, on the particulr aircraft, the model designation number was in close proximity to the radio call numbers, so that the numbers could be seen from the ground, with the wings folded or unfolded, the additional Bureau Number was omitted. If the radio call numbers were fewer than the full Bureau Number, due to space limitations, it was applied below the model designation number.

UNIT AIRCRAFT NUMBERS

Unit aircraft numerals, used to designate the number of the aircraft within the unit, consisted of numerals only. Where the Chief of Naval Operations (CNO) directives specified, the use of the last three digits of the Bureau Number was to be used as the visual identification and the aircraft within the unit marking. CNO directives permitted non-tactical aircraft to be marked with the last four digits of the Bureau number to differentiate it from another aircraft having the same last three digits. The location of the unit aircraft number was to be placed on both sides of the nose of the fuselage, utilizing a minimum size of 16 inches. Standard sizes were to be 16, 20, 24, 30 and 36 inches and, when applied, were not to exceed fifty percent of the projection of the fuselage side at the point of application. The color of this number was to be black in all cases except aircraft finished in the land camouflage scheme.

For these aircraft, size and color was left to the discretion of the Tactical Commander. The unit aircraft number was also to be placed on the upper surface of the right wing 18 inches inboard of the unit identifying letter, and on the under surface of the left wing, symmetrically located between the branch of service marking and the fuselage. Once again, this was eliminated on carrier operated aircraft and patrol aircraft with white under surfaces. Size of the numerals on the upper surface were to be 24 inches in height and on the under surface, 16 inches in height. Size and color for land camouflage aircraft was the same as above.

UNIT IDENTIFYING LETTERS

The unit identifying letter/letters, assigned to units in accordance with CNO directives, were to be applied to upper and lower surfaces of the wings and on both sides of the vertical tail surfaces. Location on the upper surface of the right wing was to be with the center of the marking placed at a distance from the wing tip equal to one-third of the distance from the fuselage to the wing tip, and in a similar location of the National Insignia on the opposite wing. On the undersurface of the right wing, the taller letters were to be located symmetrically between the National Insignia and the fuselage. Size of the letter/letters on the upper surface was to be 36 inches in height for single

Number 3 aircraft of VMF-223 on the ramp at MCAS El Toro, California, 1959. USMC

(Above) Lockheed WV-2 Constellation from AIRBARSRON-2 (Air Barrier Squadron-2) in 1959 over Diamond Head in the overall Seaplane Gray scheme. (Lockheed)

and 30 inches for doubles. Width of individual strokes were to be 4 inches. Letter/letters on the undersurface of the wings were to be 16 inches in height. These markings were eliminated from the under surfaces of carrier operated and patrol aircraft with white under wings. Location of the letter/letters on the vertical tail surface was to be above the horizontal tail surface and centered on the tail surface. Size was to be the same as for the wings, except in the case of double letters. The width could be reduced to accommodate the letters to the shape of the tail surface, while retaining maximum clarity, visibility and congruity.

In the case of shore-based aircraft, where no unit identifying letters were assigned, the name of the air station, e.g. ALAMEDA, CORPUS CHRISTI, etc., or abbreviation of the unit's title, e.g. FASRON-2, was employed in lieu of the unit identifying letter/letters. The location of these markings were the same as described in the location of the unit identifying letter/letters. On the upper surface of the right wing, the letters and numerals were to be the largest that could be accommodated on the aircraft and selected from the sizes of 12, 16, 20, 24, 30 or 36 inches. On the under surface of the right wing, the letters and numerals were to be 16 inches in height. If needed, due to space limitations, station names could occupy two lines. If two lines were used, the dash was omitted and the letters on the after line were to be centered symmetrically behind the forward line which was to contain the first syllable. The station name was also applied to the vertical tail surface, location and size the same as mentioned for the location of the unit identifying letter/letters, and above. In the event that the station name appeared on the vertical tail surface, it was not applied to the fuselage. This case referred mainly to transport aircraft.

(Above) F3D-2Q of VMCJ-3 illustrates the application of the Light Gull Gray and Insignia White scheme to this type of aircraft. The Light Gull Gray extends to nearly mid-fuselage. April 1958. (Clay Jansson)

SQUADRON DESIGNATION COLOR CODE

Squadron designation markings within carrier Air Groups consisted of the following colors on the spinner(s), and approximately the top 7 inches of the vertical tail surface(s) on both sides above the unit identifying letter(s).

1st Squadron or Unit	Glossy Insignia Red
2nd Squadron or Unit	Glossy Orange-Yellow*
3rd Squadron or Unit	Glossy Light Blue
4th Squadron or Unit	Glossy International Orange*
5th Squadron or Unit	Glossy Light Green
6th Squadron or Unit	Glossy Black*
Composite Squadron	Glossy Maroon**

All aircraft except transports were allowed to carry a squadron designation, which were optional additional markings, on the fuselage of the aircraft. Location was just forward of the empennage on both sides, and centered under the branch of service marking. Size was to be one-half the size of the branch of service marking as in **SR-2G,Amendment One** of 12 May 1950.

*Change from SR-2h
**Additional

Coast Guard Grumman UF-2G Albatross on patrol over the North Atlantic in 1959. This plane, attached to the US Coast Guard Air Detachment at Argentia, Newfoundland, still carries Orange Yellow wing tips, fuselage band and tip of vertical tail over basic Aluminum paint scheme. (USCG)

McDonnell F2H-3 Banshees from NAS Oakland, California in 1958 carrying the NAVY/MARINE Reserve marking adopted in March of 1955. "7F" indicates Oakland. (Eric Lundahl via Harry Gann)

TRANSPORT AIRCRAFT

All markings for transport aircraft remained the same as **SR-2h**, except for a few additions of letter sizes. These were added to accommodate the larger aircraft being constructed. Branch of service markings were increased so that sizes now read, 12, 16, 20, 24, 30 and 36 inches.

RESERVE AIRCRAFT

The only major change in US Naval Reserve and US Marine Corps Reserve aircraft from **SR-2h** was that the branch of service markings on aircraft jointly operated by the two services were allowed to read NAVY/MARINE at the discretion of the cognizant commands. The word MARINE was to be centered symmetrically below the word NAVY; both words being of the same letter size.

All other aircraft markings, Search and Rescue, Instrument Training etc., remained the same as described in **SR-2h**.

Under **MIL-I-18264**, all aircraft, equipped with radios were required to carry radio call numbers, consisting of not less than the last four digits of the serial number. These were to be applied to both sides of the vertical stabilizer and rudder assembly, or to each outboard side, as applicable. On rotary wing aircraft, or where space was limited, these numbers were to be applied aft along the fuselage, or aft along each side of the tail boom, as applicable. Size of the numbers was to be the largest size possible, selected from the following standard sizes: 12, 16, 20, 30 or 36 inches.

LIGHTER-THAN-AIR AIRCRAFT

All lighter than air aircraft were to carry the following markings.

The branch of service marking consisted of the words U.S. NAVY for all craft assigned to regular service functions, and the words U.S. NAVAL RESERVE for Reserve craft. The location of these words was to be on both sides of the envelope in such a manner that the letters were centered about the intersection of the horizontal axial plane and the line of the maximum diameter. Letters were to read from forward, aft on the left side and from aft, forward on the right side. Letters were to be 54 inches in height.

The model designation and serial number was to appear on both sides of the car, beginning at a point approximately twenty percent of the length from the forward end of the car with the horizontal centerline of the lettering at approximately seventy-five percent of car height as measured from the bottom of the fairing. Lettering and numerals were to be 4 inches in height.

The unit identifying letters and numerals were to be placed on both sides of the vertical fin and centered with respect to that surface. Where the empennage was oriented at forty-five degrees from the horizontal and vertical positions as in the form of an "X" or inverted "Y", these markings were placed on the lower fins, both sides, and were not to appear on any of the movable control surfaces. Letters and numerals were to be 40 inches in height.

Airships that were assigned to air stations or shore units in which no unit identifying letters and numerals had been assigned, the station name, e.g. LAKEHURST, or an abbreviation of the unit's title was affixed to both sides of the lower vertical fin. Under the station name or unit abbreviation, the serial number of the airship was placed symmetrically. Station names and the unit abbreviations were to be 15 inches in height and the serial numbers and letters 24 inches long.

Identification numbers, under **Technical Note No. -54 Conf.**, were to consist of letters and numerals to identify the following features of the airship:

PG-2/975C2N

1. The manufacturer (G in the above example denoted Goodyear Aircraft Corporation).
2. The class of airship (P in the above example).
3. The displacement of the envelope (975 in the above example denoted the displacement of 975,000 cubic feet in units of 1000 cubic feet).
4. The type of fabric in the envelope (C in the above example denoted cotton).
5. The fabric construction (2 in the above example denoted the number of piles).
6. The type of coating material on the envelope fabric (N denoted neoprene).

Location of these markings were along the line where the car met the envelope and was to be 3 inches in height for letters and numerals.

The markings covering airships has been previously mentioned throughout the text, but not in detail, and the same manner for location and size also appears in **SR-2h**.

MISCELLANEOUS MARKINGS OTHER THAN IDENTIFICATION

Miscellaneous markings under **MIL-I-18464s(Aer)** were as follows:

Propeller Tip Warning Stripe

Both sides, Glossy Orange-Yellow on the front face and camouflage* Orange Yellow on the rear face 4 inches from the tip. On propellers that had a basic diameter of more than 15 feet, the stripe was to be 6 inches from the tip. This stripe could be omitted from patrol aircraft where propeller locations were such that they produced no hazard to personnel.

Fuselage Propeller Warning Stripe and Signs

Same as **SR-2h**

Jet Engine Intake Warning Chevrons and Signs

The areas of the leading edge of the wing, or the areas of the fuselage, or the areas of the nacelle or pod, or combination thereof, which were adjacent to the sides of the jet engine intake, were marked with the following chevrons and signs. The chevron was to be applied so that the ends of their outer sides contacted the edge of the intake at points which were three-quarters of the diameter or three-quarters of the short axis of the intake port. The outer points of the chevron were to be located at a distance of 4 feet outboard along the leading edge of the wing, or forward or aft, if applied on the fuselage, or aft, if applied on the nacelle or pod, from the center of the intake. The chevrons were to be 3 inches in width and painted Glossy Insignia Red. Superimposed on one side of the chevron was the word JET, and on the other side the word INTAKE in Insignia White, in letters 2 inches in height. The word DANGER, with an arrow pointing in juxtaposition to the point of the chevron, and an arrow pointing in juxtaposition to the point of the chevron, DANGER where applied along the leading edge of the wing, or on the fuselage, nacelle or pod as applicable. Letters and arrows were marked in Insignia Red, superimposed on an Insignia White stripe 3 inches in width. Height of the letters were 2 inches. The above dimensions were to be adhered to in general, however, they could be varied, and the words DANGER with the arrows required pointing to the edge of the intake could be applied within the V of the chevron, if warranted, due to space limitations and other considerations.

*Camouflage means the same as "flat" or Non-Specular".

Walkways and Steps

In all cases where they would not contrast with the color of adjacent areas, walkway areas were to be bounded by a camouflage black line for a light background, 1/2 inch wide and marked with the word WALKWAY at sufficiently frequent intervals to indicate the walkway area. Steps were to be suitably indicated at all points on the aircraft.

Bomb Bay, Hatch, etc., Exit Warning Stripe and Signs

On all aircraft where bomb bays, hatches or other openings exit within 6 feet of each side of the propeller disc, and which could be used as means of egress (leaving) from the plane, and there was danger of personnel walking into the propellers after leaving such openings, warning stripes and signs were to be placed as follows, to definitely warn personnel regarding the proximity of propellers: those interior areas of the fuselage, bomb bay flaps, etc., which are in the plane of the propeller disc, shall be marked with Glossy Insignia Red stripes, three inches wide, extending on both sides from the center of the fuselage to the lowest extremity of such exit when open. The word PROPELLER reading vertically from top to bottom, on both sides shall be superimposed on this stripe in Insignia White letters, two inches in height, at sufficiently frequent intervals to indicate dangerous areas. The sign:

BEWARE PROPELLER ——> <—— BEWARE PROPELLER

shall be applied perpendicular to and centered with respect to the word PROPELLER, one sign on each side thereof with the arrow pointing toward the stripe. The letters and arrows shall be Glossy Insignia Red and shall be superimposed on a stripe of white, 3 inches in width. Height of the letters and length of the arrows shall be 2 inches.

Helicopter Tail Boom Warning Marking

Covered in **SR-2h**

Helicopter Rotor Blades

Main rotor blades-unmatched sets - Glossy Orange Yellow stripes were applied to the blade, both sides, from the tip to 6 inches from the tip.

Main rotor blades-matched sets - individual identification stripes were painted on both sides of the blades, from the tip to 2 inches from the tip. Stripes consisted of Glossy Insignia White for the tip of the first blade, Insignia Red for the second, and Glossy Light Green for the third. In addition, a Glossy Orange Yellow warning stripe was applied to the inboard of the 2 inch stripe on both sides extending from a line 2 inches from the tip to a line 8 inches from the tip.

Tail rotor blades were finished from the top and on both sides of the blade as follows:

(a) A 6 inch wide band of Bright Red (ANA-169).
(b) A 6 inch wide band of Glossy Insignia White (ANA-511).
(c) A 6 inch wide band of Bright Red (ANA-619).
(d) A Non-Specular Black band (ANA-604), to within 6 inches of the hub.
(e) A 6 inch wide band of Bright Red (ANA-619.

Wing Tip Tank Fins Warning Markings

Covered in **SR-2h**

Emergency Escape Markings

For transport aircraft (VR), the emergency escape panels were outlined on the exterior and interior of the aircraft with yellow reflector tape 1 inch in width. This was in accordance with **MIL-R-13689 Reflectorized Sheeting**. Emergency escape panels on patrol aircraft were marked in the same manner on the interior only. The tape was to be applied in an L-shape on each corner, and was to extend 3 inches in each direction. Larger width tape, in an appropriate color up to 2 inches, could be used as supplementary warning markings on other aircraft as long as it did not constitute a deviation from the camouflage schemes specified in **MIL-C-18263(Aer).**

Instrument Static Opening Markings

These openings were not to have any finish applied to within a 1 inch diameter circle around the opening. A Red 1/2 inch wide circular band was applied around the unpainted area. Adjacent to the marking, the following legend was applied: INSTRUMENT STATIC OPENING - DO NOT COVER.

Wing Fold Warning Flag

All aircraft with folding wings were to have these flags applied, and they were to be Red in color.

Individual ASW Helicopter Identification Marking

Individual helicopters assigned to ASW missions were to have large side and bow markings applied for visual identification. These markings were to consist of one-digit or two-digit numerals as prescribed by the cognizant commands, applied to the bow and on each side of the fuselage. Size was to be the largest possible, but not to exceed 48 inches in height except when two-digit numerals were used. They could be reduced proportionately, if space limitations or other considerations required. These markings could not interfere with any other markings already mentioned within this specification.

Helicopter Tail Rotor Guards and Stabilizers

All helicopters with tail rotor guards or stabilizers carried warning markings to prevent ground personnel from accidentally running into these components. The marking consisted of 2 inch alternating stripes of Glossy Orange-Yellow (ANA-614) and Bright Red (ANA-619).

All other markings such as lift points, hand grips, electrical connections, baggage compartments, emergency equipment, etc., were marked with the appropriate wording.

The following specifications, drawings and publications of then current issue formed a part of this specification:

SPECIFICATIONS

MIL-I-6140	Insignia; National Aircraft
MIL-I-6140	Identification of Escape Hatches, Design Requirements for
MIL-I-6143	Insignia and Markings for Search and Rescue Aircraft Design, Requirements for
MIL-F-7179	Finish and Coating; General Specification for Protection of Aircraft and Aircraft Parts
MIL-M-7911	Marking, Identification of Aeronautical Equipment, Assemblies, and Parts
MIL-D-8634	Decalomanias; For Use On Exterior Surfaces of Aircraft
MIL-P-8651(Aer)	Plates; Identification and Modification (For Aircraft), Installation of
MIL-R-1174(TC)	Painting, Marking and Insignia for US Army Aircraft, General Specification for
MIL-R-13689	Reflectorized Sheeting, Adhesive (Retro-Reflective)
MIL-C-18187(Aer)	Coating, Protective; For Fabric Surfaces of Aircraft, Application of
MIL-C-18263(Aer)	Colors; Exterior, Naval Aircraft, Requirements for
MIL-F-18264(Aer)	Finishes; Organic Aircraft, Application and Control of
MIL-S-19722(Aer)	Stencil, Marking, Paper, Pressure-Sensitive
MIL-M-25047(USAF)	Markings for Airplanes and Airplane Parts

These are just a few of the various documents that were prepared and issued for the painting and marking of US Naval and Marine Corps aircraft, and gives one a small picture of the enormous amount of paper work involved.

All colors are according to the **Air Force-Navy Aeronautical Bulletins, No. 157 Colors; List of Standard Aircraft Camouflage and No. 166 Colors; List of Standard Aircraft Glossy.**

(Above) Lockheed P2V-4 Neptune of Airborne Early Warning Squadron-3 (VW-3) in 1958. Five hurricane symbols are painted just below pilot's cockpit window signifying five flights through the 'eye' of a hurricane. This Neptune is still in the overall Glossy Sea Blue paint scheme. (Lockheed)

(Below) P2V-6 Neptune from NAS Glenview, Illinois in overall Semi-gloss Seaplane Gray. Reserve band of International Orange is partially visible just forward of the horizontal stabilizer. The "7V" tail code indicates NAS Glenview. (Eric Lundahl via Harry Gann)

This Glenview P2V-6 carries the Fluorescent (High Visibility) Color Configuration scheme called out in MIL-C-18263(Aer) of 12 February 1959. Semi-gloss Fluorescent Red Orange was added to empennage, wing tips and forward section of aircraft for Hi-Viz. Balance of this Neptune's scheme is Insignia White fuselage top surfaces and Semi-gloss Seaplane Gray lower surfaces. (Eric Lundahl via Harry Gann)

DIRECTOR, NAVAL AIR EXPERIMENTAL STATION

In a letter to the Chief, Bureau of Aeronautics (AE-422), labeled **XM-44-JO:ke, J20-1 (5175)** and dated 14 March 1956, the Director, Naval Air Experimental Station, Naval Air Material Center, Philadelphia, Pennsylvania, had just completed a series of new ANA color cards for replacement of ones already in use. It was stated in the letter that, *four hundred and fifty of the following itemized color standards are being forwarded under separate cover as enclosed (1) in accordance with the verbal request of a Bureau of Aeronautics representative (Mr. S. Kaplan).* These new color standards were:

ANA Number	Color	Quantity
605	Glossy Insignia Blue	150
614	Glossy Orange Yellow	150
619	NS Bright Red	150

The reasons for these new color standards are explained in the following letter:

BUREAU OF AERONAUTICS LETTER Aer-AE-422/85, 12 April 1956

This Bureau letter accompanied two copies of the above mentioned color standards that were distributed to all concerned parties involved with either the construction or overhauling and repairing of Naval aircraft. These new colors were issued to correct an inherent deficiency of the aeronautical paints. The new colors eliminated the undertones in the previous standard which, for matching purposes required added Red tint in the No. 605 Glossy Insignia Blue and thereby promoted bronzing, and added White tint in No. 614 Glossy Orange Yellow, No. 619 NS Bright Red which promoted discoloration and chalking. The changes in shade were minor. These new color standard cards replaced those then in use under **ANA Bulletin No. 157c** of June 1949.

MIL-C-18263A(Aer) 16 July 1956

This MIL Spec was issued on 16 July 1956, replacing **MIL-C-18263(Aer),** dated 23 February 1955. Only the changes will be noted as all paint schemes have been covered in either **SR-202 or MIL-C18263(Aer)**

HIGH VISIBILITY COLOR SCHEME

The first notable change between the two documents of **MIL-C-18263(Aer)** and **MIL-C-18263A(Aer)** was the addition of aircraft that were to be painted in the High Visibility color scheme. All aircraft mentioned in the previous **MIL spec.,MIL-C-18263(Aer),** with the addition of primary seaplanes used in training, were to be painted overall Glossy Orange Yellow, except for anti-glare panels, which were painted Non-Specular Black. Other multi-reciprocating engine and jet aircraft used in training were to carry the Glossy International Orange and Glossy International White color scheme described previously. In the instance where certain aircraft models were used by both the Training Command and Operating Command, all were to carry the Glossy International Orange and Glossy Insignia White paint scheme. In addition to the aircraft already mentioned in **MIL-C-18263(Aer),** the AF-2W, AF-3, AD-3, AD-4, S2F-1, F9F-1, F9F-8T, F2H-2, FJ-2, F9F-5, F9F-6, and T2J-1 were added to the list of aircraft that were required to carry the *Hi-Viz* paint scheme of Glossy International Orange and Glossy Insignia White.

P2V-7 (Polar Equipped) of VX-6 in Hi-Viz scheme of Fluorescent Red Orange and Semi-gloss Seaplane Gray. (Eric Lundahl via Harry Gann)

HIGH VISIBILITY COLOR SCHEME FOR TEMPORARY USE

The High Visibility paint scheme could be applied to aircraft on a temporary basis, if the aircraft operated in an area of high density air traffic, or were shore-based in the Continental United States or its possessions, and were painted in the carrier scheme. Use of this temporary color scheme had to be with the approval of the applicable Command. Application of this paint scheme consisted of using a temporary removable International Orange paint, **Specification MIL-16884**, over the existing paint scheme in the same areas as delineated in the split scheme in **SR-202**. This resulted in a modified *split* color scheme of NS Light Gull Gray and Glossy International Orange on the upper surfaces, and Glossy Insignia White and Glossy International Orange on the lower surfaces. After removal of the temporary paint, if needed, an application of the two original colors could be applied, using not more than one thin coat, otherwise cracking of the entire finish could result during subsequent service.

SOLAR HEAT REFLECTION PAINT SCHEME

Added to **MIL-C-18263A(Aer)** was the application of the Solar Heat paint scheme for advanced seaplane models used by both the Training Command and Operational Commands, the White solar-reflecting finish could be applied locally at the option of the Training Command.

SPECIAL COLOR REQUIREMENTS

When the need existed in special cases for high visibility schemes, solar-heat reflecting fuselage roof finishes, etc., such schemes were applied when specifically authorized by the Bureau of Aeronautics. Determination of local needs, and the request for it remained the responsibility of the local Commander.

LANDING GEAR

Retractable landing gear, inner surfaces of landing gear well covers, and hydro-skis were painted Glossy Insignia White. Outer surfaces were painted to match the exterior surface of the prescribed aircraft, same as **MIL-C-18263(Aer)**.

PROPELLER ASSEMBLIES

Blades were to be painted Non-Specular Black. Spinners were to be painted Non-Specular Black, except for those aircraft that were painted in the land camouflage scheme.

WING LEADING EDGE SLATS

This was a new addition of painting instructions from **MIL-C-18263f(Aer)**, and called for the interior surfaces and inboard end of wing leading edge slats and the wing area covered by the slat, when in a fully retracted position, to be painted Glossy Insignia Red. Exterior surfaces were to match the prescribed color scheme of the aircraft.

WALKWAYS AND STEPS

When anti-skid material was applied, the color of the anti-skid material was to be as follows: Walkways of landplane transports were to be Non-Specular Dark Gull Gray, except for transport aircraft finished in the high visibility paint scheme, which were NS Black. Walkways on carrier aircraft were NS Light Gull Gray. Walkways on trainers were NS Black. On aircraft finished in the special patrol plane scheme, and patrol aircraft, the walkways

(Above) VP-9 squadron insignia and the application of the 'E' award for efficiency in A-armament; B-bombing and R-rocketry. 16 May 1959. (William T Larkins)

(Above) Beech SNB-5 (4720) of VF(AW)-3 at NAS North Island, San Diego, California on 29 August 1959. 'Bugsmasher' carries the early Hi-Viz scheme of Glossy International Orange and Glossy Insignia White first ordered for use in mid-1953. Vertical tail surfaces are Insignia Blue with Orange Yellow lightning bolt, White lettering and Orange Yellow stars. (Bude Donato)

were either NS Seaplane Gray or NS Black. Walkways and steps were to be outlined in NS Black, except for aircraft painted in the target towing, drone control or land camouflage paint scheme. Also, for those aircraft finished in Seaplane Gray on the upper surfaces. Reference was to be made to **MIL-I-18464(Aer)**, in each instance for walkway markings.

ENGINE COWLING INTERIORS

The interiors of engine cowlings were to be painted Glossy Aircraft Gray.

HELICOPTER BLADES, HUBS, TRANSMISSIONS AND MOTOR MECHANISMS

The upper surface of main rotor blades remained NS Light Gull Gray, as in **MIL-C-18263(Aer)**, except for the main rotor blades of Marine Corps helicopters, which were painted NS Olive Drab, as well as the hub. If the main rotor blades on these helicopters were of wooden construction, then the color was to be NS Light Gull Gray. The lower surfaces of the main rotor blades on all helicopters were to be painted NS Black. Reference was to be made to **MIL-I-18264(Aer)**.

Transmissions and rotor mechanisms of helicopters, other than the blades and hubs, were painted Glossy Aircraft Gray. Overpainting of these items to achieve a match to the overall color scheme in the case of land camouflage scheme, arctic scheme, etc., was permitted, subject to the provisions of **Specification MIL-F-18264(Aer)** for the control of adhesion and the thickness of the individual paint coatings.

JET AIR INTAKE DUCTS

The color of the adjacent aircraft exterior was to be carried around the lip of the duct and partially into the duct except for the chevrons. The latter is described in **MIL-I-18464(Aer)**. All remaining surfaces of the duct were to be colored Glossy Insignia White.

ENGINE EXHAUST AREAS

Exterior surfaces which were significantly impinged upon by the exhaust gas were to be considered as engine exhaust areas and were painted as follows: On transports and utility aircraft, Glossy Aircraft Gray. On Trainers and combat type aircraft finished in the overall Semi-Glossy Seaplane Gray color scheme, Glossy Engine Gray. Combat type reciprocating engine aircraft assigned to training use, Glossy Engine Gray. On all other aircraft, engine exhaust areas conformed to the color scheme of the aircraft.

LANDING GEAR STRUTS, WHEEL ASSEMBLIES, ETC.

Retractable landing struts, wheel assemblies, brake housings, etc., were painted Glossy Insignia White.

POLISHED AREAS

Polished, unpainted areas were left on the inboard side of the engine nacelles and wing tip tanks, as required, to permit observation from the cockpit of the position of the landing gear, bomb bay doors, etc.

COLOR SCHEMES

The only major change in color schemes from **MIL-C-18263(Aer)** was that of Marine Observation Landplanes, land camouflage color scheme, in which these aircraft, formally painted NS Olive Drab and Glossy Insignia White, would now be painted NS Field Green.

Slight changes in the color scheme application were noted in the carrier color scheme. The erosion-resistant finish now extended back to a line approximately 3 inches from the leading edge, as measured to the leading edge in the chord plane. Previously, this finish had been carried to the first row of rivets. Also appearing for the first time was the addition of the painting of the jet air intake ducts and the lips of the ducts, already explained in **MIL-I-1846A**. Glossy Insignia White was to be used for all MAD* housings, except on the frontal areas requiring rain erosion resistant coatings, and on all rockets, rocket launchers, other accessories, equipment and weapons attached to the under surface of the airframe.

MIL-C-18263A(Aer) AMENDMENT-1 30 July 1957

Under this amendment to **MIL-C-18263A(Aer)** there were several minor changes that were incorporated into the painting document that covered Naval and Marine Corps aircraft.

HIGH VISIBILITY COLOR SCHEME

Added to the list of aircraft to be painted Orange Yellow were individual HUP-2 and H04S-3 helicopters used in training. A new sub paragraph was added, stating that for special conditions which arise, other than those already cited, the local command was authorized to use the following paint scheme; either Glossy International Orange, Glossy Insignia White, or Glossy International Orange/Glossy Insignia White/Light Gull Gray.

*Magnetic Anomally Detector

Under the temporary high visibility scheme, all helicopters finished in the NS Light Gull Gray color scheme could carry the following scheme applied locally when authorized by the Type Commander: Application of International Orange temporary removable paint, **Specification MIL-P-6884**, over the existing color scheme except for the areas that require extensive masking. Such areas should be left '*as is*'. With the diverse configurations and sizes of then present and planned helicopters, the Bureau of Aeronautics did not establish any standard patterns of *split* or *modified split* color schemes for helicopters, as was done for fixed winged aircraft.

Another change in the *Hi-Viz* paint scheme was for jet aircraft. On the split of the Glossy International Orange and Glossy Insignia White of the wings, a two inch white border was now incorporated around the National Insignia on the portion that extended into the Glossy International Orange.

ANTI-GLARE PANELS

This change incorporated the addition of one word — *airborne,* which stated all piloted aircraft would carry the anti-glare panel on all *airborne* surfaces which would produce glare in the pilot's or co-pilot's eyes.

PROPELLER ASSEMBLIES

Propeller blades, under **Amendment 1**, would not have to be painted NS Black if the following conditions were met. (1) Corrosion protection is not required and (2) the blades are so situated as to produce no glare or excessive brightness in the pilot's or co-pilot's eyes; e.g., in cases where the blades rotated in a plane aft of the pilot's seat. If these conditions were not met, the blades were to be painted NS Black.

TRANSMISSIONS AND ROTOR MECHANISMS OF HELICOPTERS

The color of the transmissions and rotor mechanisms were changed from Glossy Aircraft Gray to Engine Gray.

COLOR SCHEMES

The following color schemes were changed by **Amendment 1**, which had been the same since **MIL-C-18263(Aer)**.

All warning aircraft (VW), landbased, with normal operating altitudes greater than 15,000 feet, would now be painted Glossy Aircraft Gray, except for the top of the fuselage which was to carry the solar-reflecting finish.

Warning aircraft, landbased, that operated at less than 15,000 feet retained their overall Semi-Gloss Seaplane Gray Color scheme, while those operating from carriers remained the same NS Light Gull Gray and Glossy Insignia White.

The following helicopters, HU, HC, HO, HR and HS, were now painted Glossy Engine Gray instead of NS Light Gull Gray.

Douglas A4D-1 Skyhawk of Headquarters and Maintenance Squadron 12 in formation with a Grumman F9F-8P Cougar of Marine Composite and Photographic Squadron 3 in August of 1959. Both aircraft are painted in the Light Gull Gray over Insignia White scheme with the H&MS-12 Skyhawk in Red trim colors with White stars. Anti-glare panels differ; the Cougar has a Black panel while the Skyhawk has one of Medium Green. (Clay Jansson)

North American FJ-4B Fury (143516) from VMA-223 featuring White trim with Red lightning bolts. (USMC via Rowland P Gill)

MIL-I-18464A(Aer) 28 MARCH 1957

All items covered in **MIL-I-18464(Aer)** of 9 March 1955 remained the same in this document with no noticeable changes or additions.

On 28 May 1957, the Chief of Naval Operations, in a re-organization of the Naval Air Reserve program, directed that seventy-three Auxiliary Air Units located throughout the country be decommissioned during the next six months.

MIL-I-18464A(Aer) AMENDMENT-1 9 August 1957

For this amendment to **MIL-I-18464A(Aer)**, only one change was incorporated into the document. This change called for the addition of the words ABANDON CHUTE to be applied to the bottom of the fuselages of all search and rescue helicopters, in an appropriate location, so as to be readily visible from below. The lettering was to be the largest possible size which could be accommodated on the helicopter and selected from the standard sizes of 12, 16, 20, 24, 30 and 36 inches.

Also, in the month of July 1957, two changes in Naval Aviation were initiated. One was that after the establishment of the Single Manager for Airlift Service, the Fleet Logistic Air Wings were abolished and transport squadrons not assigned to the Single Manager Service were redesignated Fleet Tactical Support Squadrons (VR), and reassigned to operate directly under the control of Fleet Commanders. Secondly, the Air Force Pacific Fleet, and Air Force Atlantic Fleet, were retitled and became Naval Air Force, Pacific Fleet, and Naval Air Force, Atlantic Fleet.

As Naval Aviation moved into the year 1958, a new concept of carrier warfare became apparent for the future. On 4 February the keel of the world's first nuclear powered aircraft carrier, USS ENTERPRISE, was laid at Newport News, Rhode Island.

On 13 February a selected Reserve was set up within the overall Reserve Organization to provide fully trained and equipped forces and units for direct and immediate deployment to specific active duty assignments upon the commencement of hostilities. The entire Naval Air Reserve was incorporated into this new organization.

With the indoctrination of the new Reserve Organization, the structure of Naval Aviation was as follows:

The Replacement Air Group (RAG) system, was divided into four sections:

RCVG	-	Replacement Carrier Air Group
VAH	-	Heavy Attack Squadron Training Program
RCVSG	-	Replacement Carrier Antisubmarine Air Group
RVP	-	Replacement Patrol Squadron

Depending upon the classification a graduating Naval aviator had during his training, either in operational ASW, or in operational attack, he would be sent to one of the above replacement squadrons or air groups.

ATTACK RAGs consisted of:

Atlantic Fleet RAG RCVG-4		Pacific Fleet RCVG-12	
VAH-3	VA-44	VA-122	VF-121
VA-42	VF-101	VA-125	VF-124
VA-43	VF-101 Detachment A	VA-126	VAH-123
	VF-174	VA-127	

HEAVY ATTACK SQUADRON RAGs

ATLANTIC FLEET	PACIFIC FLEET
VAH-3*	VAH-123**

Atlantic Fleet	Pacific Fleet
RCVSG-50	RCVSG-51
VS-30	VS-41
HS-1	HS-10

PATROL RAGs

Atlantic Fleet	Pacific Fleet
Fleet Air Wings Atlantic	**Fleet Air Wing Fourteen**
VP-30	VP-31

On 10 March, the CNO approved a reorganization of carrier aviation that would create uniform Air Groups, provide a more permanent group assignment to ships, and permit a reduction of assigned units and aircraft without also reducing combat readiness. The new organization also provided for a permanent replacement Air Group to be established on each Coast which was made responsible for the indoctrination of key maintenance personnel, the tactical training of aviators, and for conducting special programs required for the introduction of new models of combat aircraft.

On 21 April, the CNO directed that assigned Navy squadrons be organized into Naval Air Transport Wings, one for the Pacific and one for the Atlantic. This was done to clarify command relations and to permit a closer integration of Naval units into the Single Manager Airlift Service.

MIL-I-18464B(Aer) 30 September 1958

On 30 September 1958, **MIL-I-18464B(Aer)** was issued to all Navy Commands and interested contractors. This document was the same as the previous one, **MIL-I-18464A(Aer)**, except that now the amendment of 9 August 1957 was included.

Carrier Air Groups received new tail letter codes.

Former Letter	New Letters	Unit	Former Letter	New Letters	Unit
T	AB	CVG-1	H	NL	CVG-15
M	NE	CVGl-2	R	AL	CVG-17
K	AC	CVG-3	B	NM	CVG-19
F	AD	CVG-4	G	NP	CVG-21
S	NF	CVG-5	U	NA	ATG-1
C	AF	CVG-6	W	NB	ATG-2
L	AG	CVG-7	Y	NC	ATG-3
E	AJ	CVG-8	Z	ND	ATG-4
N	NG	CVG-9	I	AM	ATG-181
P	AK	CVG-10	O	AN	ATG-182
V	NH	CVG-11	J	AP	ATG-201
D	NJ	CVG-12	X	AQ	ATG-202
A	NK	CVG-14			

*VAH-3 Operated under Heavy Attack Wing One.
**VAH-123 operated under RCVG-12 ASW CARRIER RAG

Douglas F3D-2Q Skyknights of VMCJ-2 on the line at MCAS Cherry Point, North Carolina. The High Visibility color scheme for temporary use has been applied. Basic scheme is Light Gull Gray over Insignia White with International Orange added to the wing tips, forward fuselage and rudder. (USMC via Rowland P. Gill)

Identification Letters assigned to Naval Aircraft units.

FIGHTER (All Weather)

VF(AW)-3	TT	VF(AW)-4	GC

LIGHT PHOTOGRAPHIC

VFP-61	PP	VFP-62	GA

CARRIER AEW

VAW-11	RR	VAW-12	GE

ALL WEATHER ATTACK

VA(AW)-33	GD	VA(AW)-35	VV

HEAVY PHOTOGRAPHIC

VAP-61	SS	VAP-62	GB

HEAVY ATTACK

VAH-1	GH	VAH-6	ZC
VAH-2	ZA	VAH-7	GL
VAH-3	GJ	VAH-8	ZD
VAH-4	ZB	VAH-9	GM
VAH-5	GK	VAH-11	GN

ANTI-SUBMARINE

VS-21	YA	VS-32	MD
VS-23	PF	VS-36	ME
VS-27	MA	VS-37	SU
VS-30	MB	VS-38	ST
VS-31	MC	VS-39	MF

HELICOPTER-ANTI-SUBMARINE

HS-1	HA	HS-6	UB
HS-2	SK	HS-7	HD
HS-3	HB	HS-8	VB
HS-4	TA	HS-9	HE
HS-5	HC	HS-11	HF

PATROL

VP-1	YB	VP-9	PD	VP-22	QA	VP-45	LN
VP-2	YC	VP-10	LD	VP-23	LJ	VP-46	RC
VP-4	YD	VP-11	LE	VP-26	LK	VP-47	RD
VP-5	LA	VP-16	LF	VP-28	QC	VP-48	SF
VP-6	PC	VP-18	LG	VP-40	QE	VP-49	LP
VP-7	LB	VP-19	PE	VP-42	RB	VP-50	SG
VP-8	LC	VP-21	LH	VP-44	LM	VP-56	LQ

HEAVY ATTACK (Mining)

VA(HM)-10	ZE	VA(HM)-13	LR

AEW MAINTENANCE

AIRBARSRON-2
SH (Air Barrier Squadron-2)

AIRBORNE EARLY WARNING

VW-1	TE	VW-11	MJ
VW-2	MG	VW-12	SJ
VW-3	PM	VW-14	VA
VW-4	MH	VW-15	ML

AIR TRANSPORT

VR-1	JK	VR-21	RZ
VR-2	RA	VR-22	JL
VR-3	RT	VR-24	JM
VR-6	JR	VR(F)-31	JN
VR-7	RN	VR(F)-32	JP
VR-8	RH		

ELECTRONIC COUNTERMEASURE

VQ-1	PR	VQ-2	JQ

UTILITY

VU-1	UA	VU-6	JG
VU-2	JE	VU-7	UH
VU-3	UF	VU-10	JH
VU-4	JF	HU-1	UP
VU-5	UE	HU-2	HU

AIR DEVELOPMENT

VX-1	JA	VX-4	XF
VX-2	JB	VX-5	XE
VX-3	JC	VX-6	JD

AIRSHIP

ZP-2	KP	ZW-1	KE
ZP-3	KE		

MISCELLANEOUS

CMGRU-1	ZZ	(Counter Measures Group-1)
CMGRU-2	GC	(Counter Measures Group-2)
FAETULANT	HJ	(Fleet Airborne Electronics Training Unit, Atlantic)
FAETUPAC	PB	(Fleet Airborne Electronics Training Unit, Pacific)
FAWTULANT	HG	(Fleet All-Weather Training Unit, Atlantic)
FAWTUPAC	PA	(Fleet All-Weather Training Unit, Pacific)
SWULANT	HL	(Special Weapons Unit, Atlantic)
FAGUPAC	TR	(Fleet Air Gunnery Unit, Pacific)
HATULANT	HK	(Heavy Attack Training Unit, Atlantic)
HATUPAC	ZG	(Heavy Attack Training Unit, Pacific)

FLEET AIR SERVICE SQUADRONS

FASRON-2	FA	FASRON-101	FH	FASRON-108	FP
FASRON-3	FB	FASRON-102	FJ	FASRON-109	FQ
FASRON-5	FC	FASRON-104	FK	FASRON-111	FR
FASRON-6	FD	FASRON-105	Fl	FASRON-121	FS
FASRON-9	FE	FASRON-106	FM	FASRON-200	FT
FASRON-51	FG	FASRON-107	FN	FASRON-201	FU

Identification Letters Assigned to Fleet Marine and Marine Support Units

HEADQUARTERS

AIRFMFPAC	WZ	(Aircraft, Fleet Marine Force, Pacific)
H & HSLANT	BZ	(Headquarters and Headquarters Squadron, Atlantic)
H & MS-10	SE	(Headquarters and Maintenance Squadron)
H & MS-11	TM	
H & MS-12	WA	
H & MS-13	YU	
H & MS-14	CN	
H & MS-15	YV	
H & MS-16	WW	
H & MS-20	BT	
H & MS-24	EW	
H & MS-26	EL	
H & MS-31	DV	
H & MS-32	DA	
H & MS-33	WM	
H & MS-35	BM	
H & MS-36	WX	

FIGHTER

VMF(AW)-114	EK	VMF-323	WS
VMF(AW)-115	VE	VMF-333	DN
VMF-122	DC	VMF-334	WU
VMF-232	WT	VMF-451	VM
VMF-235	DB	VMF(AW)-513	WF
VMF-251	DW	VMF(AW)-531	EC
VMF-312	DR	VMF(AW)-542	WH
VMF(AW)-312	VW		

ATTACK

VMA-121	VK	VMA-225	CE
VMA-211	CF	VMA-311	WL
VMA-212	WD	VMA-324	DX
VMA-214	WE	VMA-331	DP
VMA-223	WP	VMA-332	VL
VMA-224	WK	VMA-533	ED

AIRCRAFT REPAIR

MARS-17	SZ	MARS-37	QF
MARS-27	CZ		

OBSERVATION

VMO-1	ER	VMO-6	WB
VMO-2	VS		

COMPOSITE AND PHOTOGRAPHIC

VMJ-1	YW	VMCJ-2	CY
VMC-1	RM	VMCH-3	TN

TRANSPORT

VMR-152	WC	VMR-253	QD
VMR-153	BC	VMR-352	QB
VMR-252	BH	VMR-353	DZ

HELICOPTER TRANSPORT

HMR(L)-161	YR	HMR(L)-YN	
HMR(L)-162	YS	HMR(L)-362	YL
HMR(L)-163	YP	HMR(L)-363	YZ
HMR(L)-261	EM	HMR(L)-461	CY
HMR(L)-262	ET		

HELICOPTER DEVELOPMENT

HMX-1

MISCELLANEOUS

VMFT-10	SA	(Marine Fighter)
VMFT(AW)-10	SC	inactive
VMIT-10	SD	(Marine Instrument Training Squadron)
VMAT-10	SB	inactive
VMFT-20	BF	
VMFT(AW)-20	BP	(Marine All-Weather Fighter Training Squadron)
VMIT-20	BE	
VMAT-20	BY	(Marine Attack Training Squadron)

These aircraft letters were assigned in the following manner:

COMMAND	FIRST CHARACTER	SECOND CHARACTER
ComNavAirLant	A through M	A through Z
ComNavAirPac	N through Z	A through Z
CNATRA	2 through 9	A through Z

MIL-C-18263B(AER) 12 February 1959

MIL-C-18263B(Aer), superseding **MIL-C-18263A(Aer)**, was issued by the Bureau of Aeronautics on 12 February 1959, and was virtually the same as the previous document with the addition of the amendment of 30 July 1957 and a few minor changes.

ANTI-SUBMARINE WARFARE AIRCRAFT

All anti-submarine aircraft, except carrier based, now employed the white solar-reflecting fuselage roof and were finished in the color of overall Semi-Gloss Seaplane Gray, except for the aforementioned roof. The Glossy Insignia White of the top surface extended down to the line of maximum width of the fuselage, and faded out in the vicinity of the tail cone. The blending of the two colors produced a sharp, or masked line. Aircraft affected by this change were the P5M, P2V, and P3V.

FLUORESCENT (HIGH VISIBILITY) COLOR CONFIGURATIONS

All four engine and two engine transport landplanes in the Naval air establishment, which operate predominately within the United States, were to be painted with the Semi-Gloss Fluorescent Red Orange color scheme. Application of the paint scheme was as follows: wing tip markings on the top and bottom of the wings extended inboard on the wings to the aileron cutout, but excluded the ailerons, flaps, and trim tabs; the entire tail section, excluding rudders, elevators and trim tabs and an area extending forward on the fuselage to the zone where the vertical stabilizer faired into the fuselage, which provided at least a 9 foot length of fluorescent paint; also the bottom and the sides on the front elevators and trim tabs and an area extending forward on the fuselage to the zone where the vertical stabilizer faired into the fuselage, which also provided at least a 9 foot length of fluorescent paint; also the bottom and the sides on the front portion of the fuselage, starting from the radome (if any), and extending aft to a line perpendicular to the leading edge of the wing on two engine transports, or aft to a line perpendicular to the most forward portion of the engines on four engine transports. The fluorescent paint on the front of the fuselage extended to the white solar-reflecting top, while on the rear of the aircraft, a half circle or crescent shape was formed on the side of the fuselage, forming a peak or point on the top and bottom. The national insignia markings, solor-reflecting finish, anti-glare, walkway materials, rain-erosion resistant finish, de-icer boots, exhaust tail finish, etc., retained their original color. A margin, not exceeding 2 inches, was left between the fluorescent finish and national insignia. Transports used for research and development, test and related support mis-

Patrol Squadron 47's Martin P5M-2 Marlin nose section illustrates application of the Glossy Insignia White over Semi-Gloss Sea Gray, US national insignia, individual aircraft numeral, propeller warning stripe and a rather clever arrangement of efficiency award letters. 20 August 1960 (William T Larkins)

Lockheed R7V-1 Constellation "PHOENIX" of VX-6 with Arctic top color scheme of Semi-Gloss Seaplane Gray paint. A thin White line between top color and natural metal fuselage is evident. Tail group is painted with Hi-Viz Fluorescent Red Orange with the moveable surfaces being painted Aluminum. (Eric Lundahl via Harry Gann)

sions were included in the above mentioned paint scheme. Transports used for Fleet logistic support and early warning were exempted. All fixed winged aircraft assigned to search and rescue work, and patrol type aircraft assigned to training use, carried the same *high-viz* paint scheme as the two engine transports.

All training, proficiency and utility aircraft were painted in accordance with the following fluorescent paint scheme. For reciprocating engine trainers and utility aircraft, using the SNB as an example, the paint scheme was as follows: on the upper and lower surface of the wings the fluorescent paint was applied to the rear one-half of the wing, including the ailerons and trim tabs. The upper portion of the horizontal stabilizer was Semi-Gloss Fluorescent Red Orange, except for the aileron and trim tabs, while the other half remained the color of the aircraft, in this case, Glossy Insignia White. The vertical stabilizers, both sides, were Red Orange, including the rudders and trip tabs. The Semi-Gloss Fluorescent Red Orange also extended forward from the tail section and formed the same shape as described for the transport scheme. The lower half of the fuselage was also painted Semi-Gloss Fluorescent Red Orange, the color being terminated on the bottom with a line parallel to the line of Red Orange on the rear half of the wings.

For jet aircraft, the same scheme was followed, except on the fuselage where the Semi-Gloss Fluorescent Red Orange extended from the tail surface, a perpendicular line was formed; not the half circle or crescent shape.

Helicopters, such as HTs, HUP-2s and HO4S-3s, used in training were painted all over Semi-Gloss Fluorescent Red Orange, except for areas that required extensive masking and anti-glare areas.

Radomes were not to be painted Semi-Gloss Fluorescent Red Orange over any existing paint.

LANDING GEAR

Under the section of colors for landing gear, a new portion was added from the previous painting document governing wheel doors. The insides remained Glossy Insignia White, but now carried a Glossy Insignia Red color on the edges of the doors. The Red was to be applied without smearing onto the Glossy Insignia White.

The major paint scheme changes for aircraft that appeared in **MIL-C-18263B(Aer)** are listed below.

Transport Landplanes (VR)	Aluminum G Insignia White/Semi-Gloss SG Fluorescent Red Orange
Transport Seaplanes (VR)	SG Seaplane Gray SG Fluorescent Red Orange
Trainer (Landplane) (VT)	G Insignia White
Single Reciprocating Engine	SG Fluorescent Red Orange
Multi-reciprocating Engine	G Insignia White SG Fluorescent Red Orange
Trainer (Seaplane) (VT)	
Advanced	G Insignia White
Primary	SG Fluorescent Red Orange
Trainer (Jet) (VT)	
Intermediate	G Insignia White
Basic	SG Fluorescent Red Orange
Primary	
Warning (VW)	
Landbased, normal operating altitudes greater than 15,000 feet	G Aircraft Gray and G Insignia White
KD Target (KD)	SG Fluorescent Yellow Orange
Target Drone (K)	SG Fluorescent Yellow Orange

MIL-C-18263B(Aer) AMENDMENT 1 30 April 1959

In this first amendment to **MIL-C-18263B(Aer)**, there were major changes involving the schemes of aircraft that were painted with the fluorescent finish.

FLUORESCENT (HIGH VISIBILITY) COLOR CONFIGURATIONS

Added to the list of aircraft that were finished in the Semi-Gloss Fluorescent Red Orange scheme were all helicopters assigned to search and rescue work.

The fluorescent paint scheme was not applied to the control surfaces of any aircraft except in the following cases: Utility training and carrier type aircraft on which the entire horizontal tail is movable, such as the F8U Crusader. In the case of the latter, the entire horizontal tail surface was painted Semi-Gloss Fluorescent Red Orange where applicable. Utility, training and carrier type aircraft, such as the SNB/JRB, on which the rudder was more than twenty-five percent of the area of the combined rudder and stabilizer, both the rudder and stabilizer were painted with the fluorescent finish.

For single reciprocating engine trainer or utility aircraft, such as the SNB, the Semi-Gloss Fluorescent Red Orange paint scheme was reversed. Instead of the rear portion of the wings being painted with the fluorescent finish, the paint scheme was now reversed, and the forward one-half of the wing was finished with the Semi-Gloss Fluorescent Red Orange. On the top half of the wing, the Semi-Gloss Fluorescent Red Orange was terminated at the engine nacelles with the outer half of the nacelles remaining Glossy Insignia White. The inboard side of the nacelle was painted in the anti-glare color, NS Black, and the Semi-Gloss Fluorescent Red Orange was continued, terminating at the fuselage. The Semi-Gloss Fluorescent Red Orange on the lower half of the wing extended from wing tip to wing tip, across the fuselage, and excluding the engine nacelles. The entire lower portion of the fuselage was Semi-Gloss Fluorescent Red Orange, terminating half way up on the sides. Tail surfaces remained the same as in **MIL-Cl-18263B(Aer)**.

The Semi-Gloss Fluorescent Red Orange finish on jet aircraft was reversed in the same manner, except that now ailerons, trim tabs and horizontal stabilizers on the tail section were painted Glossy Insignia White.

HIGH VISIBILITY COLOR SCHEME FOR TEMPORARY USE

Added to this section was that after the application of the Semi-Gloss Fluorescent Orange/White color scheme, the Gray, or NS Field Green of the basic camouflage color scheme was not to be visible except for small areas requiring extensive masking. These areas retained the basic aircraft color scheme for ease of applications.

The last addition to **MIL-C-18263B(Aer)** under this amendment called for Utility aircraft to be painted in the Semi-Gloss Fluorescent Red Orange/Glossy Insignia White color scheme.

In September of 1959, airship flights by Reserves of the Naval Air Reserve Training Unit, Lakehurst, marked the end of the airship training program which had been conducted for twelve years under the Chief of Naval Air Reserve Training. The Airship Training Group at the Naval Air Station, Glynco, Georgia was the first group decommissioned, ending the lighter-than-air training for the United States Navy, on 2 November 1959.

Boeing PB-1G still serving the Coast Guard in 1960. Fuselage band is Orange Yellow outlined in Black. The placement of the US National insignia is unusual but occasionally seen on Coast Guard aircraft. This PB-1G was based at Elizabeth City, North Carolina at this time. (USCG)

MIL-C-18263B(Aer) AMENDMENT 2, 7 December 1959

This second amendment to **MIL-C-18263B(Aer)** dealt with several changes in color schemes for aircraft, but the most significant change noted was that the number of the basic specification **MIL-C-19263B(Aer)** was changed to read **MIL-C-18263B(Wep)**. All documents that followed would now become (Wep) specs.

TEMPORARY PAINT

The first major change in the specification was that the word *temporary* was changed to read removable, and the addition of Semi-Gloss Seaplane Gray or Semi-Gloss Black color to modify a solar reflecting White roof for artic operations was adopted.

ANTI-SUBMARINE WARFARE AIRCRAFT

Helicopters (HSS-1, HSS-2 and HSS-1N) used in anti-submarine operations were now to be finished in the Semi-Gloss Fluorescent Red Orange color scheme. This scheme consisted of the nose of the helicopters carrying a fluorescent finish to terminate at a line drawn from the lower forward corner of the pilot's window (closed portion) on the HSS-1, and HSS-1N, and drawn from the center of the lower edge of the pilot's side window (closed portion) in the case of the HSS-2. This border line was parallel to the pylon fold hinge. The fluorescent finish on the pylon covered the area from the pylon fold hinge line aft and terminated a sufficient distance below the top of the pylon to permit the application of identification letters and numerals on the background Gray of the basic color scheme. Transparent areas, openings, screens and any portion of the exhaust trail and anti-glare areas were not painted with the Fluorescent finish. Hull bottoms, including an area 6 inches above the full load water line, were exempted from the Flourescent finish. This included such aircraft as the P5M-2 and all UF type aircraft. Also, all areas finished with rain erosion resistant finish were exempted from the Fluorescent finish.

Amendment Number 2 also produced slight changes in the Fluorescent paint schemes for reciprocating trainer and utility aircraft. Using the SNB as an example, the Semi-Gloss Fluorescent Red Orange finish on the upper portion of the wing was still applied to the forward one-half of the wing. It now included the outer portion of the engine nacelle, the remaining half of the nacelle, or inside,being an anti-glare color; in this case NS Black. The Semi-Gloss Fluorescent Red Orange was now terminated on the outer side of the engine nacelle and did not cover the portion from the inboard side of the engine nacelle to the fuselage. On the lower or bottom portion of the wings, the Semi-Gloss Fluorescent Red Orange now included the lower portion of the engine nacelles, excluding the cowlings. The remainder of the aircraft was painted in accordance with the previously mentioned Mil spec. and amendment.

TOWING AND AERIAL TARGET CONTROL AIRCRAFT COLOR SCHEME

Amendment Number 2 changed the color scheme for drone control aircraft. The vertical fin which had been previously painted Glossy Orange Yellow was changed to Semi-Gloss Fluorescent Red Orange. The rudder and wing bands that had previously been painted Glossy Insignia Red were now painted Semi-Gloss Fluorescent Red Orange.

MIL-I-18464C(Wep) 11 April 1960

This Mil spec. was the same as **MIL-I-18464B** with the exception of the American flags which were to be applied to certain aircraft. The American flag that carried forty-eight stars was to be replaced with one of forty-nine stars. The American flag consisting of fifty stars would replace the ones of forty-nine stars after 4 July 1960.

On 1 May 1960, seventeen Basic Training Groups of the Naval Air Training Command were redesignated Training Squadrons (VT), and placed in commission as separate units, each under the command of a commanding officer.

MIL-I-18464C(Wep) AMENDMENT 1 16 August 1960

Under this amendment, the specifications for the sizes of the fifty star American flag was incorporated with a complete breakdown of standard proportions as to length and width.

SOUTH VIETNAMESE MARKINGS

Also included in this amendment was the addition of plates depicting the markings for the National Insignia for South Vietnam. The National Insignia for South Vietnam was the same as incorporated on US Navy aircraft except that the Glossy Insignia White bars were painted Glossy Orange-Yellow and the Glossy Insignia Blue border was painted Glossy Insignia Red. The star and field remained their respective colors of Glossy Insignia White and Insignia Blue. This amendment also stated that South Vietnamese aircraft would carry a tail flash emblem consisting of Glossy Orange-Yellow and Glossy Insignia Red and a fighter insignia on the nose of the aircraft. For the fin flash, the top one-quarter was to be colored Glossy Orange-Yellow, the mid one-half would be equal bands of Glossy Orange-Yellow and Glossy Insignia Red with the remaining one-quarter being colored Glossy Orange-Yellow.

The color schemes and marking specification remained unchanged until the end of 1961.

LIGHTER THAN AIR TERMINATION

On 21 May 1961, the Secretary of the Navy approved plans for the termination of the lighter-than-air program. These plans decommissioned all operational units by the end of November, and placed eight of the ten remaining airships in storage. The Overhaul and Repair Facility at Lakehurst was inactivated, leaving another page of history filled. On 31 October, Fleet Airship Wing One and Patrol Squadrons ZP-1 and ZP-3, the last operating units of the LTA branch of Naval Aviation, were decommissioned at Lakehurst.

While this segment of Naval Aviation was being brought to an end in 1961, another phase of Naval Aviation history was being launched. On 25 November, USS ENTERPRISE (CVAN-65) the Navy's first nuclear-powered aircraft carrier was commissioned at Newport News, Virginia.

Last hurrah for the non-rigid airship, the Goodyear built ZPG-3W built for the Navy's early warning radar network. This 1960 photo illustrates the Aluminum neoprene coated envelope with U.S. NAVY lettering, 54 inches high, and Non-specular Light Gull Gray painted car. (Goodyear)

MIL-C-18263C(Wep) 27 December 1961

The first major change in this specification was that of the application of removable paint. Materials available under specification **MIL-P-6884**, paint, temporary identification could be applied over the permanent paint finish by field activities when authorized by the applicable command, and when the use of a permanent paint finish for obtaining the prescribed color configuration was not advisable, such as in the following cases:

Land camouflage

On aircraft that were finished in the Semi-Gloss Seaplane Gray color, addition of Glossy Insignia White to surfaces viewed from below, for camouflage against sky backgrounds.

Addition of temporary markings and seasonal color schemes.

Obliteration of existing markings for special missions.

Addition of Semi-Gloss Seaplane Gray or Semi-Gloss Black color to modify a solar reflecting Glossy Insignia White roof for Arctic operations.

Addition of Semi-Gloss Seaplane Gray to cover the White roof of aircraft in operations near unfriendly forces.

CARRIER AIRCRAFT

A Slight change in the painting of carrier aircraft appeared as the vertical control surfaces were now painted Glossy Insignia White. Until this time, they had been painted NS Light Gull Gray with only the horizontal control surfaces being painted Glossy Insignia White.

Carrier type aircraft models used in both Training and Operating Commands retained their combat color scheme when issued from overhaul or new production. The high visibility color scheme was applied locally on such aircraft when they were used in training and/or when authorized by the Chief of Naval Air Training. Carrier type aircraft assigned exclusively to training use were issued from overhaul or new production with the high visibility Semi-Gloss Fluorescent Red Orange and Glossy Insignia White color scheme.

BASIC COLOR SCHEME

Under **MIL-C-18263C(Wep)**, slight changes were made in the following paint schemes:

Search and Rescue (VU) Seaplanes	G	Insignia White
	SG	Seaplane Gray
	SG	Fluorescent Red Orange
Submarine Search (HS) Seaplanes	G	Insignia White
	SG	Seaplane Gray
	SG	Fluorescent Red Orange
Submarine Search (HS) and Attack	G	Engine Gray
	SG	Fluorescent Red Orange
KD Target (KD)	G	Insignia White on upper surfaces, (except fuselage); vertical stabilizer,rudder.
	SG	Fluorescent Yellow-Orange on entire fuselage
	G	Insignia Red on bottom of all aerodynamic surfaces
Drone, Anti-Submarine (DS)	G	Engine Gray
	SG	Fluorescent Red Orange
	SG	Fluorescent Green. Color was Engine Gray except for Red Orange on left side; Fluorescent Green on right side.

FLUORESCENT (HIGH VISIBILITY) COLOR CONFIGURATIONS

Once again, this MIL spec called for slight changes in the high visibility paint schemes for Navy and Marine Corps aircraft. Authority was granted to extend the high visibility fluorescent color to the entire exterior surface of helicopters intended for service deployment in remote areas. In special cases such as the HTL and HUL helicopters, painting was balanced so that the weight of paint forward of the helicopter was balanced by the weight of paint aft.

The general principles applicable to the placement of the Semi-Gloss Fluorescent Red Orange paint were as follows:

a. Wing tip markings on the top and bottom of the wings, extending inboard on the wings about one-third of the length of each wing, but extending inboard no less than 4 feet nor more than 8 feet. Unless specific dimensions were given, the fluorescent strip was terminated at the natural break in the wing contour, and horizontal control surfaces were not painted with the fluorescent paint. The entire vertical tail section to the zone where the vertical stabilizer flared into the fuselage was painted Semi-Gloss Fluorescent Red Orange. Control surfaces were not painted if a rebalancing of these surfaces would be necessary due to the addition of the Semi-Gloss Fluorescent Red Orange. This paint scheme was mostly used by transports, both two and four engines, and the crescent or halfmoon configuration already mentioned, remained in existence on these aircraft.

b. For all aircraft, except transports, the bottom and sides of the front portion of the fuselage, starting from the radome, if any, and extending aft and terminating at a line perpendicular to the forward edge of the front canopy, was painted Semi-Gloss Fluorescent Red Orange. For transports, the areas receiving this paint were the bottom and sides on the front portion of the fuselage, starting from the radome, if any, and extending aft to a line perpendicular to the leading edge of the wing on two-engine transports, or aft to a line perpendicular to the most forward portion of the engines on four engine-transports. The customary insignia, rain erosion resistant finish, de-icer boots, exhaust tail finish, etc., retained their original colors, and were not painted with the Semi-Gloss Fluorescent Red Orange finish and the National Insignia, and the edges of the Fluorescent finish were sanded smooth, when dry, to avoid any aerodynamic disturbance.

The Semi-Gloss Fluorescent Red-Orange areas on reciprocating engine trainers and jet trainers were changed once again. Instead of the split high visibility paint scheme, these aircraft now carried the following scheme:

a. One third of the wing area was to be painted Semi-Gloss Fluorescent Red Orange, the one-third area being that area starting from the tip of the wing and extending inboard.

b. The entire vertical tail section, including rudders and trim tabs, to the zone where the vertical stabilizer flared into the fuselage was finished in the fluorescent finish, with the requirements of rebalancing control surfaces, after the application of the finish being enforced under **MIL-P-21698**.

c. The fluorescent finish was not applied to the leading edges of the wings, stabilizers, tip tanks, belly tanks, radomes, etc., of these aircraft.

Lockheed EP-2E (P2V-5FE) Neptune (127777), attached to NAS Glenview, Illinois. Colors are Insignia White top of fuselage; while the wings, lower fuselage and engine nacelles are Semi-gloss Seaplane Gray. (Eric Lundahl via Harry Gann)

EXAMPLES OF
SQUADRON INSIGNIAS

VT-17
1946

VF-9A
1947

VA-25
1949

VF-113
1950

VMF-121
1951

VF-21
1951

VF-13
1952

VA-155
1953

VMA-251
1954

VA-85
1955

VA-42
1956

VA-76
1957

VA-65
1958

VF-101
1958

VA-215
1962

VA-15
1964

VA-115
1965

VA-176
1966

VF-162
1970

VF-11
1974

VF-31
1975

VF-74
1977

VMA-211
1977

VF-84
1978

VF-213
1984

The wing tip tanks on aircraft that carried the fluorescent finish, such as the P2V, were painted Semi-Gloss Fluorescent Red Orange all over, except for the anti-glare and polished areas, and the leading edges as stated above. The fluorescent finish was not applied to any transparent or translucent plastic, or metal frames or fittings on aircraft windows. The fluorescent finish was not applied to the nose sections of any aircraft having an area of less than 2 square feet, such as the F8U Crusader.

SEARCH AND RESCUE SCHEME

The description of this color scheme for Search and Rescue aircraft appeared for the first time in a **MIL-C-Spec**. Previously these aircraft had been mentioned in the **MIL-I-1643 Specifications**.

Under **MIL-C-18263C(Wep)**, Search and Rescue aircıaft were painted in the following manner: On each side of the forward part of the fuselage, centered between the leading edge of the wing and bow, or nose, a rectangle, whose length was equal to three times its height, appeared in Orange Yellow. The height of the rectangle was thirty-three percent of the vertical dimension of the projection of the fuselage side at the point of application, except that the height of the rectangle was not larger than 36, nor less than 20 inches, including the border which was Glossy Black. The rectangle was located as near as possible to the center of the vertical projection of the fuselage at the point of application. The base of the rectangle was parallel to the longitudinal axis of the fuselage.

Using the P5M as an example, the following locations of colors were as follows: The Orange Yellow rectangle, as mentioned before, was located on the forward portion of the fuselage. Also a Glossy Orange-Yellow band, outlined in Glossy Black, was located just forward of the vertical tail surface, starting just above the water line and extending over the top of the fuselage to the other side, ending just above the water line. This band was 36 inches wide, and the black border was 3 inches wide. The upper portion of the wing, between the outer edges of the engine nacelles was painted Glossy Orange-Yellow with a Glossy Black border, the Glossy Orange-Yellow not extending onto the cowling covers and ending at the rear of the leading edge finish. The floats were painted Glossy Orange-Yellow, including the float strut. The wing tips and the vertical tail surfaces were painted Semi-Gloss Fluorescent Red Orange in the same manner as transport aircraft already mentioned. The basic colors of the P5M, as mentioned above, were Semi-Gloss Seaplane Gray wth a Glossy Insignia White solar reflecting top.

Search and Rescue helicopters were painted in Semi-Gloss Fluorescent Red Orange and Glossy Engine Gray, and did not carry any of the Glossy Orange-Yellow markings as described above.

PROPELLER ASSEMBLIES

Propeller blades on multi-engined planes were painted on both sides from the tip to 3 inches from the tip with Glossy Insignia White, followed by a 6 inch strip of Glossy Insignia Red, then a 3 inch strip of Glossy Insignia White. The remainder of the blade was painted NS Black on both sides. However, the NS Black was eliminated on the blades if the following two conditions were met. First, if corrosion protection was not required, and secondly, if the blades were so situated that they did not produce glare or excessive brightness in the pilot's or copilot's seat, e.g., in cases where the blades rotate in a place aft of the pilot's seat. If the blades were so situated as to produce glare or excessive brightness in the pilot's or copilot's eyes, the Glossy Insignia Red and the Glossy Insignia White were replaced with NS Bright Red and NS Insignia White, respectively, on the rear face of the blades only. Propeller blades on single engined planes were painted on the front side in the same manner as for multi-engine blades; the rear face, however, shall be colored NS Black.

The only other significant change in **MIL-C-18263C(Wep)** was the addition of paint schemes for tail rotor blades and main rotor blades for helicopters. These markings, up until this time, had appeared in **MIL-I-18464** specs.

Many changes had taken place throughout the years 1954 to 1961 in the field of aircraft color schemes; the first in 1955 when the Glossy Sea Blue color was phased out and the Glossy Insignia White and NS Light Gull Gray color became the major combat color scheme for US Navy and Marine Corps aircraft.

Since the truce had been signed in Korea, tensions had created an uneasy situation in the Far East and the Middle East. These tense situations kept both the Sixth and Seventh Fleets in constant readiness.

New carriers, missiles and aircraft were introduced as the years continued. Old ships and aircraft were phased out to make room for the new, and Naval and Marine Corps Aviation marked its golden anniversary in 1961, and CDR Alan B Shepard, USN, became the first American in space.

As the United States moved into the early 1960s, a new era in the field of aviation was about to unfold and was born with the coming of the space age.

More than half of the nation's first astronauts had Navy backgrounds; beginning with CDR Alan B Shepard, USN, who made the United States' first trip into space with a sub-orbital flight on 5 May 1961. LT COL John H Glenn, USMC, became the first American astronaut to orbit the earth on 20 February 1962.

On 31 August 1962, the last flight of a Navy airship took place at Lakehurst, New Jersey, ending a forty-five year era of lighter-than-air operations, that had started with the DN-1, the Navy's first airship.

On 18 September 1962, a joint Army-Navy-Air Force regulation was issued, establishing a uniform system of designating military aircraft, similar to that previously in use by the Air Force. Under this regulation, all existing aircraft were redesignated using a letter, dash, number and letter, to indicate in that order, the basic mission or type of aircraft, its place in the series of that type, and its place in the series of that type, and its place in the series of the changes in the basic design. Under this system, the Crusader, formerly the F8U-2, became the F-8C, indicating the third change (C) in the eighth (8) of the fighter (F) series. Provision was also made for indicating the status of the aircraft and modifications of its basic mission by prefix letters. Thus, the YF8U-1P, became the YRF-8A, symbolizing a prototype (Y) of the photo-reconnaissance (R) modification of the F-8A aircraft.

Underside of a Lockheed P2V-5F Neptune illustrates the Semi-gloss Seaplane Gray and Insignia White scheme for patrol bombers per directive of 12 February 1959. 10 November 1960. (Lockheed)

(Below) Sikorsky SH-34J from NAS Glenview, Illinois carries the Glossy Engine Gray and Semi-gloss Fluorescent Red Orange paint scheme for search and rescue type post-December 1961. Tail rotor tips are painted Insignia Red/Insignia White/Insignia Red. (Eric Lundahl via Harry Gann)

McDonnell F3B (F3H-2) Demon of VF-213 after the model designation change of September 1962. Tip of vertical tail surfaces are painted Light Blue to designate the third squadron and carries Orange Yellow stars. Tail letters "NP" are 30 inches high, and are assigned to CVG-21 at this time. The constellation Leo (Lion) sign is applied with Insignia Blue paint as is the fuselage flash above the word NAVY. (Harry Gann)

(Above) Douglas A4D-2N Skyhawks of VA-144 at NAAS (Naval Auxiliary Air Station), Fallon, Nevada in 1960. Lightning bolt is International Orange designating the 4th squadron. Tip of vertical tail surface is also painted Orange. (USN)

(Below) A4D-2N Skyhawks of CVG-19's VA-192 during the modification period when vertical control surfaces were ordered painted Insignia White by MIL-C-18263C (Wep) of 27 December 1961.

MIL-C-18263C(Wep) AMENDMENT 1 20 September 1962

This first amendment to **MIL-C-19263B(Wep)** incorporated slight changes in the color schemes of related aircraft.

The first change required helicopters that had floatation hulls, and were finished in the fluorescent color scheme, would now include a tapered fluorescent stripe down the length of the hull.

PROPELLER ASSEMBLIES

Propeller blades on single engine aircraft now carried a 4 inch NS Orange-Yellow band on the rear face at the tip for all blades of less than 15 feet in diameter, and a 6 inch NS Orange-Yellow band for larger diameter blades.

FLUORESCENT PAINT SCHEMES

All aircraft used by the Fleet, and subject to recall, had a solvent removable type paint applied over the basic color scheme when attached to a Command requiring the fluorescent high visibility paint scheme.

MIL-I-18464D(Wep) 26 October 1962

This MIL specification was issued on 26 October 1962, and saw very few changes in the insignia and markings for Naval Aircraft.

Letters and numeral sizes were changed slightly, and the selection of sizes as compared to the previous list were as follows:

Letters and numerals (Old sizes)
Small l- 1, 2, 3, 4, and 6 inches in height.
Medium - 12, 16, and 20 inches in height.
Large - 24, 30 and 36 inches in height.
Letters and numerals (New sizes)
Small - 1, 2, 3, 4 1/2, and 6 inches in height.
Medium - 9, 12, 15, 18 and 21 inches in height.
Large - 24, 30, 36, 42 and 48 inches in height.

The section covering Helicopter Rotor Blades was eliminated from the Insignia and Markings specifications, and now appeared in the specification covering exterior paint schemes, i.e. **MIL-C-18263C(Wep)**.

JET ENGINE BLAST WARNING

On all aircraft, the areas of the fuselage, or the areas of the nacelle or pod, or combination thereof, which were adjacent to the sides of a jet engine exhaust, were marked with the words BEWARE OF BLAST.

EXTERNAL EXIT EMERGENCY RELEASE

Each external exit emergency release or handle was to be clearly marked by a RESCUE arrow applied on the fuselage. Application of the RESCUE marking was accomplished either by painting, or by applying a decalcomania marking. The head of the arrow was to be pointed forward, except in the case of vertical markings, and as close to the release mechanism as practical without overlapping other primary markings. Secondary markings, such as STEP or ACCESS DOOR, were omitted as required to accommodate the rescue markings.

The last addition to this MIL spec. was that if space limitations permit on tactical-type aircraft with White rudders, an effort should be made to avoid applying the unit identifying letters on the White finish. However, the specified height of the letters were to be maintained.

As of 1 November 1962, the United States Navy had reduced its attack carrier groups to fifteen. These consisted of six in the Atlantic, and nine in the Pacific.

ATLANTIC	PACIFIC
CVG-1	CVG-2
CVG-3	CVG-5
CVG-6	CVG-9
CVG-7	CVG-11
CVG-8	CVG-14
CVG-10	CVG-15
	CVG-16
	CVG-19
	CVG-21

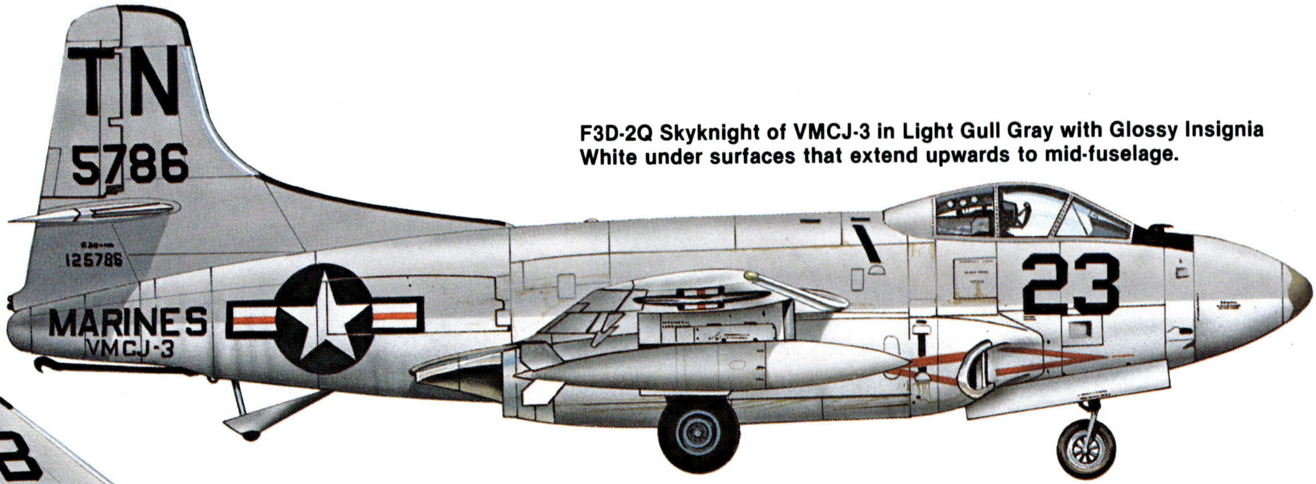

F3D-2Q Skyknight of VMCJ-3 in Light Gull Gray with Glossy Insignia White under surfaces that extend upwards to mid-fuselage.

F3H-2 Demon of VF-14 'Top Hatters' off ROOSEVELT (CVA-42) in 1961. The aircraft carries Insignia White control surfaces including the full stabilators. Red trim denotes the first squadron of CVG-1.

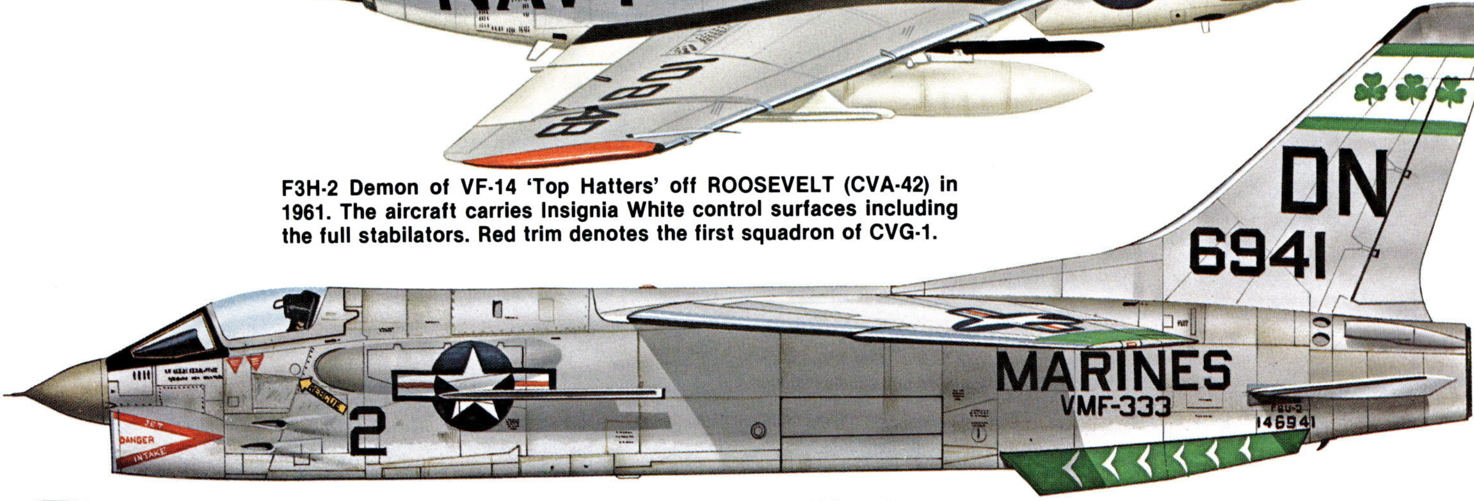

F8U-1 Crusader of VMF-333 off FORRESTAL (CVA-59). Trim colors are Light Green and White.

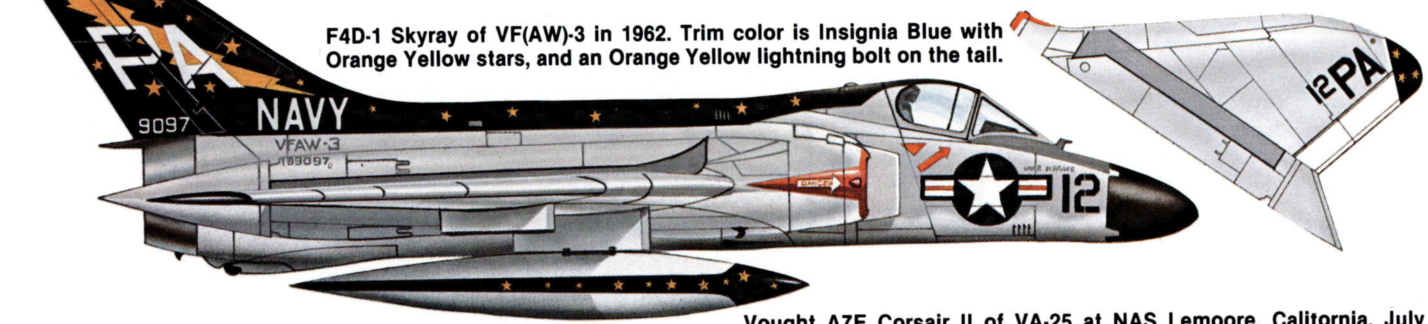

F4D-1 Skyray of VF(AW)-3 in 1962. Trim color is Insignia Blue with Orange Yellow stars, and an Orange Yellow lightning bolt on the tail.

Grumman A6A Intruder of VMA(AW)-224 at MCAS Cherry Point, NC, 1972. Rudder is Dark Green. (Jim Sullivan)

Vought A7E Corsair II of VA-25 at NAS Lemoore, California, July 1973.Tail and wing tanks are trimmed in Dark Green, the rudder and tail tips are White. (B R Jackson)

HUP-2 with a Glossy Insignia White top over Glossy Engine Gray under surfaces during 1965.

A6A Intruder of VA-42 'Green Pawns' at NAS Oceana. Green trim indicates the fifth squadron of Combat Readiness Replacement Air Group 4.

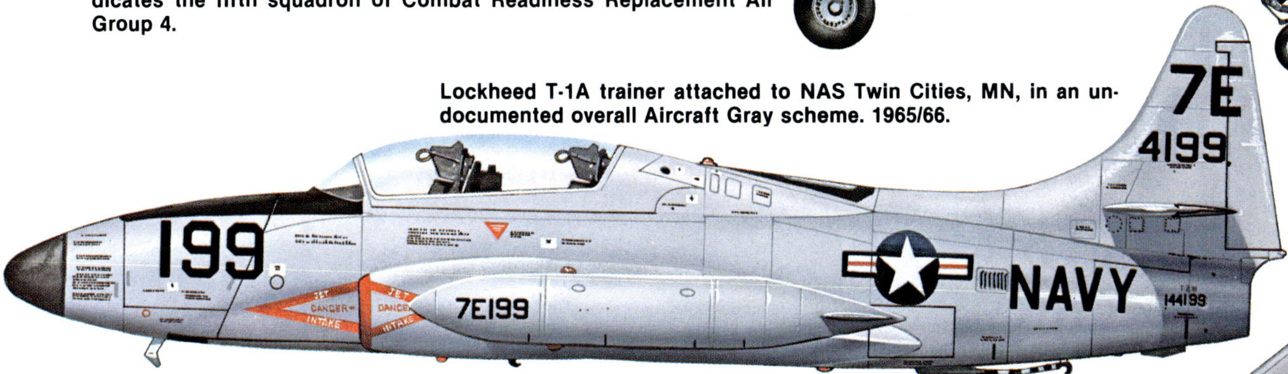

Lockheed T-1A trainer attached to NAS Twin Cities, MN, in an undocumented overall Aircraft Gray scheme. 1965/66.

A-4B Skyhawk of VMA-214 'Blacksheep', Detachment N off HORNET (CVS-12). Trim color is Black. NAS North Island 1964.

Lockheed QT-33 Point Mugu, California, 1973. (B R Jackson)

Overall Insignia White station aircraft from NARF, El Centro, California in 1961. Aircraft is North American T-28B Trojan. (USN via Harry Gann)

(Above) US Coast Guard HC-130B Hercules in flight during 1961. Fluorescent Blaze Orange paint on tail surface, wings, fuselage band and nose section is shown in very faded condition. This scheme proved unsatisfactory due to poor wearability, and was replaced by International Orange during aircraft overhauls. (USCG)

Each CVG normally consisted of two fighter squadrons, all-weather, and three or four attack squadrons. On the FORRESTAL and MIDWAY class carriers, two of the squadrons were *light* jet attack (single pilot), one squadron was *heavy attack* and one was a prop *medium* VA squadron. The ESSEX class CVAs carried two attack squadrons and a prop squadron. Some ESSEX class carriers operating in the Pacific carried a VAH detachment.

In addition to these squadrons, which normally carried from nine to fifteen aircraft each, an additional segment of aircraft were usually carried from the following detachments:

1. An early warning, or *WHISKEY* detachment, three to five aircraft from VAW-11 or VAW-12.
2. A photographic detachment, usually three aircraft from VFP-62 or VFP-63.
3. A countermeasure, or *QUEEN* detachment, of two to four aircraft from VAW-33 or VAW-13.

MIL-I-18464D(Wep) AMENDMENT 1, 8 March 1963

This first amendment to **MIL-I-18464(Wep)** saw the Military Standard 795 color code for Air Force-Navy color schemes changed to read Federal Standard 595.

On 1 April 1963, all Replacement Air Groups (RAGs) were redesignated to Combat Readiness Air Groups (CRAGs). This designation was changed to bring their title in line with their function.

(Below) Rows of Lockheed P2V-5 Neptunes in for modification during the early 1960s. Semi-gloss Seaplane Gray and Insignia White scheme is evident. Flap degree markings are Insignia Red and White. Lettering on flap degree marking reads '30 20 10' top to bottom. (Lockheed)

Grumman SHU-16B Albatross painted in special scheme for landbased seaplanes, Semi-gloss Seaplane Gray upper surfaces with Insignia White undersides. VP-31 tested the SHU-16B as an ASW vehicle for foreign use during 1961-62. (Clay Jansson)

MIL-I-18464D(Wep) AMENDMENT 2, 24 May 1963

This second amendment to **MIL-I-18464(Wep)** created only one significant change, the application of the American flag for smaller aircraft.

For the smaller aircraft, the length of the flag was not to exceed seventy-five percent of the chord at one-half of the height of the vertical tail surface from the horizontal surface. For smaller aircraft with twin vertical stabilizers, the length of the flag was not to exceed seventy-five percent of the chord at one-half the height of the vertical surface.

MIL-I-18464D(Wep) AMENDMENT 3 30 September 1963

This third Amendment to **MIL-I-18464(Wep)** created several changes to the marking of Naval aircraft.

HELICOPTER TAIL BOOM WARNING MARKING

If a permanent fluorescent paint was applied to the tail boom, the Glossy Orange-Yellow band was omitted, and the arrow and warning legend was applied in Glossy Black on the fluorescent paint. In cases where temporary fluorescent paint was used on the tail boom, the paint was applied over the Glossy Orange-Yellow band, except that the red arrow and warning legend remained visible in a rectangle of appropriate size.

UNIT AIRCRAFT NUMERAL

The minimum height of these numerals was changed from 16 inches to 12 inches.

SQUADRON DESIGNATION

The squadron designation for transport aircraft could now be applied to the aft section of the aircraft upon approval of the cognizant command. This was only permitted if space limitations would not allow the designation to be placed on both sides of the fuselage, just forward of the empennage and centered under the branch of service marking.

UNIT IDENTIFYING LETTER

The size of these letters was changed from 36 inches for single letters and 30 inches for double letters, appearing on the upper surface of the right wing, to a minimum height of 20 inches with the selection being from the following sizes: 20, 24, 30 or 36 inches, and the largest size possible. The width of the stroke of these letters, 4 inches, was deleted. The letters on the under surface of the right wing remained at 16 inches.

Unit identifying letters on the vertical tail surfaces of all aircraft were changed from a minimum height of 36 inches for single letters and 30 inches for double letters, to a minimum height of 20 inches. Selection was the same as described above, with the deletion of the 4 inch stroke.

On 20 December 1963Carrier Air Groups (CVG) were redesignated Carrier Air Wings (CVW).

MIL-I-18464E(Wep) 20 May 1964

This MIL spec., issued on 20 May 1964, saw several minor and a few major changes in the markings for Naval aircraft as well as several modifications within the document itself.

WING TIP FLOATS (P5-ONLY)

The wing tip floats on the P5 were now required to carry a one-inch white stripe on the inboard side, centered at float W. L. 20, and parallel to the load water line of the aircraft.

SEARCH AND RESCUE AIRCRAFT

The markings for search and rescue aircraft appeared for the first time in a **MIL-I-18464** specification. Up until this time, these markings had been covered under **MIL-I-6143**, although several drawings depicting aircraft with search and rescue markings had appeared in **MIL-I-18464** documents.

The search and rescue markings of **MIL-I-18464E** were as follows:

SEAPLANE AND LARGE AMPHIBIANS

Wing tip floats and struts were painted Glossy Orange Yellow.

The upper and lower surfaces of both wing tips were painted Glossy Orange Yellow from the wing tip inboard at a distance equal to seven percent of the total wing span, float included. A 6 inch black border was added inboard. The upper surface of the center section of the wing, including the rear projection portion of the engine nacelles, was painted Glossy Orange-Yellow to a distance just inboard of the two engine nacelles. A 6 inch black border was added outboard.

On the upper surface, the word RESCUE was superimposed in Glossy Black, and centered aft of the word RESCUE, the appropriate identification numerals and/or letters were added. Letters and numerals were to be 36 inches high.

A 36 inch Glossy Orange-Yellow band with a border of two 6 inch black stripes was located approximately 3 feet forward of the leading edge of the horizontal stabilizer, and encircled the aft portion of the hull.

On the forward section of the hull, a Glossy Orange Yellow rectangle whose length was equal to three times its height was painted on each side of the forward part of the hull, and centered between the leading edge of the wing and bow. A 2 inch black border was placed around the rectangle. On the bottom of the hull, between the bow and the main strip, and extending from chine to chine, were the search and rescue identification numerals and/or letters. The top of the letters and/or numbers were at the port chine of the hull and were Glossy Orange-Yellow with a 2 inch black border. Identification numbers and/or letters were 2/3 the height of the Glossy Orange-Yellow rectangle.

HELICOPTERS

Search and rescue helicopters were painted overall Glossy Orange-Yellow, and the word RESCUE painted Glossy Black was located at the widest part of the top of the fuselage, aft of the enclosure, and on the bottom of the fuselage; the largest letters possible that space would permit were used. The word ABANDON CHUTE were placed on the bottom of the fuselage in a location that would be readily visible from below. The size of the lettering was chosen from the standard sizes of 12, 16, 20, 24, 30 and 36 inches.

A-1H Skyraider carrying the temporary Medium Green over Glossy Insignia White camouflage scheme used on board the KITTYHAWK and CONSTELLATION during their Vietnam tour of 1966. The scheme was not overly successful and was discontinued at the end of the tour.

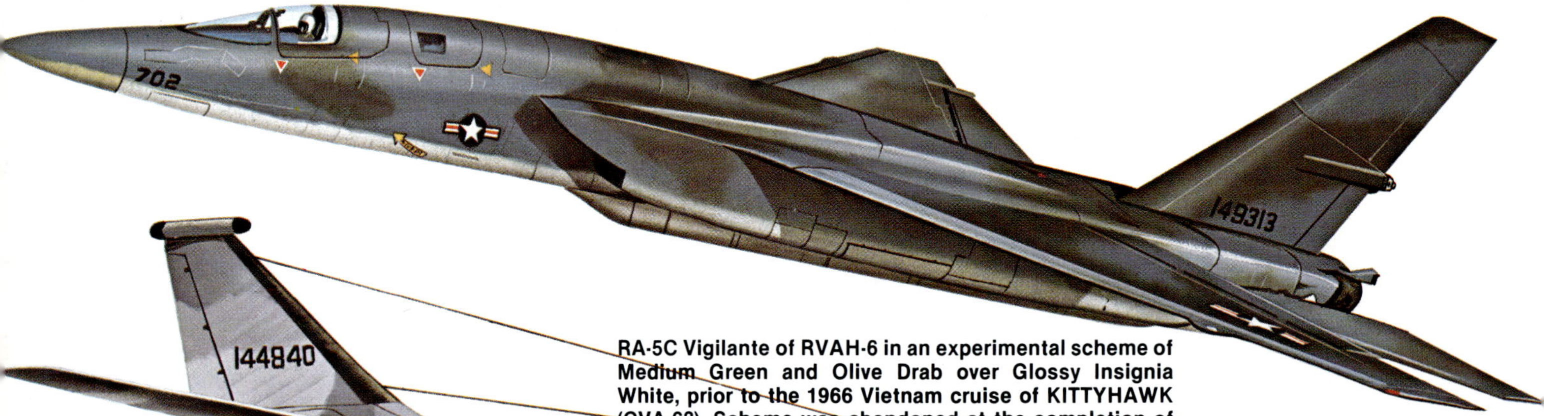

RA-5C Vigilante of RVAH-6 in an experimental scheme of Medium Green and Olive Drab over Glossy Insignia White, prior to the 1966 Vietnam cruise of KITTYHAWK (CVA-63). Scheme was abandoned at the completion of the cruise.

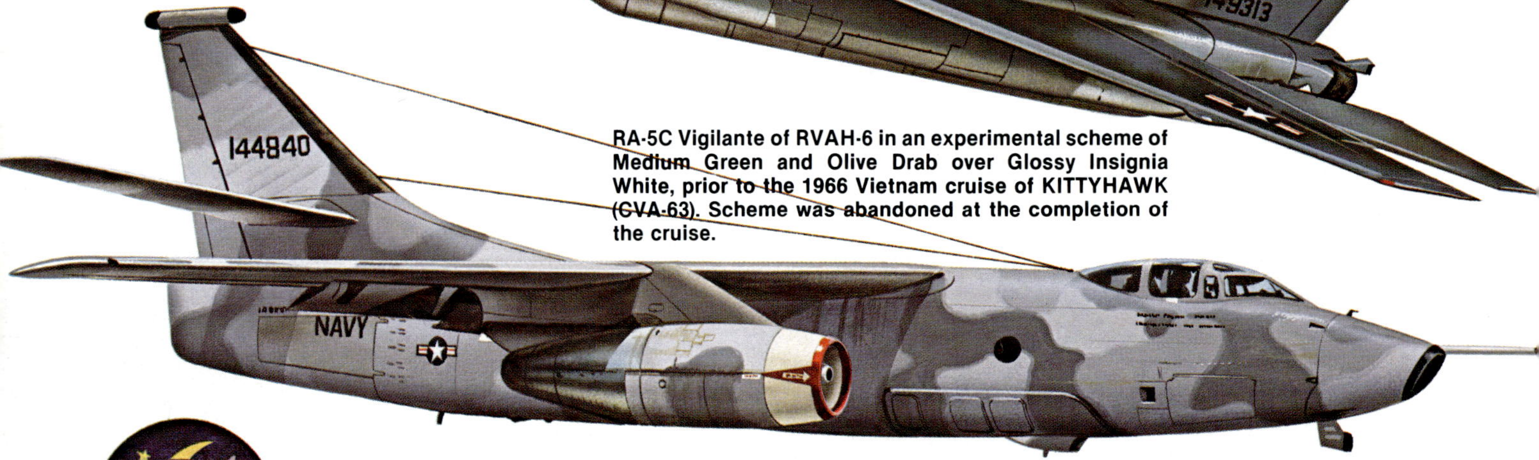

Douglas RA-3C Skywarrior of VQ-1 'Batmen' in a three Gray (FS36118, FS33631, and FS36440) scheme in 1972.

Lockheed AP-2H Neptune of Project Trim, 1968. Author Tom Doll spent a lot of time with this three toned Gray bird.

North American OV-10A Bronco of VS-41, NAS North Island, California, 1970. Insignia on nose is an Emerald Green clover leaf in a White circle. (Jerry Kishpaugh)

Marine Corps North American YOV-10D Bronco in one of the many non standard schemes deployed to Vietnam for operational testing. 1971. (George Adair)

Lockheed OP-2E Neptune of VO-67 at Davis-Monthan AFB, 1973. Upper surfaces are Medium Green (34079) over Light Gull Gray (36440) lower surfaces. (Duane Kasulka)

The experimental all Black F-4J Phantom II of VX-4, known as 'Vandy One', tested the anti-corrosiveness of the paint. 1973. (Jerry Kispaugh)

McDonnell F-4J of VX-4 at Point Mugu, California in a Light Blue and Medium Blue Experimental scheme (Jerry Kishpaugh)

Douglas A-4F Skyhawk, 'Lady Jessie' of VA-164 off HANCOCK (CVA-19), one of the more colorful aircraft in the Navy, at NAS Lemoore, California, 1974. (Jerry Kishpaugh)

Northrop F5E Tiger in various shades of Blue and Gray as part of 'TOP GUN' at NAS Miramar, California, 1975. (Jerry Kishpaugh)

Douglas A-4E Skyhawk of VMA-211, MCAS Iwakuni, Japan, 1976. (USMC via Hideki Yamauchi)

The markings, as specified for large seaplanes and amphibians, were used as appropriate to the size and shape of the aircraft.

The search and rescue markings described here, may also be found in **MIL-C-18263C**.

Several major and minor markings that had been covered in **MIL-I-18464** specifications previously were now incorporated in **Specification MIL-M-25047**. Included in this change were markings such as the fuselage propeller warning stripe and sign, jet engine intake warning chevrons and signs, walkways and steps, arresting hooks, helicopter tail boom warning stripe, wing folding flag and helicopter tail rotor guards and stabilizers.

The external exit emergency release and emergency escape marking were now covered in **Specification MIL-A-25165**.

On 1 January 1964, Fleet Air Wings Pacific was established, and on 15 January, the command Fleet Air Southwest Pacific and Fleet Air Japan were disestablished. On the same day, Carrier Divisions 15, 17 and 19 were designated Antisubmarine Warfare Groups 1, 3 and 5 respectively, and transferred from ComASWForPac for administrative control. The mission of the newly organized groups was to develop antisubmarine carrier group tactics, doctrine and operating procedures including co-ordination with patrol aircraft operations. Following this new concept of special antisubmarine divisions, an office of Antisubmarine Warfare Programs was established under the Chief of Naval Operations. This office was to exercise centralized supervision and co-ordination of all antisubmarine warfare planning, programming and appraising. This office was established on 17 February.

On 13 March, 1964, instructions were issued to redesignate all Heavy Attack Squadrons (VAH), upon assignment of RA-5C Vigilante aircraft as Reconnaissance Attack Squadrons (RVAH).

F3H-2 Demons of VF-14 on the USS FRANKLIN D ROOSEVELT (CVA-42) in 1961. These Demons carry Insignia Red trim color designating the 1st squadron. The 'Top Hat' insignia is carried in a White circle. The "AB" tail letters signify CVG-1. (USN via VF-14)

(Above) Vought F8U-1 Crusader leaves USS FORRESTAL (CVA-59) during exercises in 1961. VMF-333 squadron colors are Light Green and Insignia White. (USMC via W T Larkins)

(Below) F9F-8T Cougar trainer being readied for flight at NAS Lemoore, California on 27 October 1961. Fluorescent Red Orange and Insignia White scheme is carried. (USN)

MIL-C-18263D(Wep) 29 June 1964

The first major change in color schemes that appeared in this document was the elimination of the special patrol paint scheme. All patrol planes were now painted with a Glossy Insignia White solar reflecting fuselage roof with the remainder of the plane being finished in NS Light Gull Gray. Previously, patrol aircraft were painted in an overall Semi-Gloss Seaplane Gray paint scheme except in special cases; such as the P5M, P3V and UF. These aircraft were covered under the special patrol paint scheme of **MIL-C-18263C(Wep).**

FLUORESCENT (HIGH VISIBILITY) COLOR CONFIGURATIONS

Perhaps the biggest change in color schemes was that now, the fluorescent, high visibility, color scheme was now used only on aircraft in the Training Command, excluding Reserve Training, target control and SAR aircraft, target aircraft and drones. Requests for using the fluorescent finish on the other aircraft, or for special mission aircraft, e.g. Arctic operations, had to be submitted to the Type Commander or Controlling Custodian to the Chief of Naval Operations for approval.

For all aircraft utilizing the fluorescent paint, it was not to be applied to skids and on areas where skin temperatures were above 210 degrees F., and was not to be applied below, or within, 6 inches above the waterline of seaplanes.

SOLAR HEAT REFLECTION

All Cargo aircraft and Utility land planes were now painted with a Glossy Insignia White solar heat reflecting fuselage top. On Zulu* aircraft, a Glossy Insignia Blue stripe below the Glossy Insignia White area and a blue chevron on the nacelles could be employed for decorative purposes.

The major changes in paint schemes are listed below:

Patrol (VP)	NS	Light Gull Gray
	G	Insignia White
Transports (VR)		
Landplanes	G	Aircraft Gray
	G	Insignia White
Utility Landplanes (VU)	G	Insignia White
	G	Aircraft Gray
Utility Seaplanes (VU)	G	Insignia White
	SG	Seaplane Gray
Helicopters		
Submarine Search and Rescue	G	Engine Gray

The last major change presented in **MIL-C-18263D** was that all bare metal would now require complete painting except on the C-118 and C-131 aircraft, where the lower fuselage and vertical stabilizer were to remain bare aluminum.

Amendment Number 1 of **MIL-C-18263C(Wep)** was also incorporated into **MIL-C-18363D(Wep)** and became a part of the latter.

**Administrative-Command Aircraft*

Lockheed P2V-5F Neptune at Greenwood, Nova Scotia, Canada in June of 1962. This Patrol Squadron 44 Neptune is painted per MIL-C-18263D (Wep) of 12 February 1959. APU cart is Orange Yellow. ('d E C Darby)

(Below) Lockheed P3V-1 Orion of VP-9 in flight over San Francisco during the early 1960s. Standard patrol plane scheme of Semi-gloss Seaplane Gray and Insignia White is carried.

Douglas F4D-1 Skyray of VF(AW)-3 during 1962. Orange Yellow lightning bolt and stars decorate this 'Ford'. Anti-glare panel is Medium Green. (VF(AW)-3 via W A Riley)

(Below) Overall Fluorescent Red Orange paint covers this Sikorsky UH-34J helicopter attached to the Reserve base at NAS Willow Grove, Pennsylvania during the early 1960s. The National insignia is outlined with Insignia White. Lettering is Black. Tail rotor tips are Red/White/Red. (Eric Lundahl via Harry Gann)

McDonnell RF-4B Phantom II 'Spirit of America' of VMFP-3, MCAS Iwakuni, Japan, 1976. Color regulations went out the window as Bi-Centennial schemes began to appear. (USMC)

Marine Douglas OA-4M of H&MS-12, NAS Alameda, California,in a multi-Gray tactical scheme with Light Gray letters and numbers. May 1980. (Jerry Kishpaugh)

Northrop F-18A Hornet of VFA-125. The only vestiges of the older marking system are the Black numbers and letters on the tail, all other markings are in Medium Gray. 1981. (Jerry Kishpaugh)

Douglas TA-4J Skyhawk of VA-127, 1981. (Jerry Kishpaugh)

Vought A-7E Corsair II of VA-195, 1982 (Jerry Kishpaugh)

Douglas TA-4F Skyhawk of VA-127 in a multi-Gray tactical scheme with White lettering, September 1980. (Jerry Kishpaugh)

McDonnell F-4N Phantom II of VMFA-321 in a not completely 'toned down' scheme, 1981. (Douglas R. Tachauer)

Douglas TA-4J Skyhawk of VA-127 in Blue, Gray, and Tan at NAS Lemoore, California, 1981. (Jerry Kishpaugh)

Vought A-7B Corsair II of VA-205 at Dobbins AFB (NAS Atlanta, GA) 1982. Good example of the Tactical paint scheme. (Douglas R Tachauer)

McDonnell F-4S of VF-301 in two shades of Blue and one of Gray. Markings are in Black and Red. USN Reserve, August 1982. (Jerry Kishpaugh)

Douglas TA-4J Skyhawk of VC-12 at NAS Oceana, VA, October 1982, painted in the tactical scheme. (Douglas R Tachauer)

McDonnell F4N Phantom II of VF-171 (KW) at NAS Oceana, VA, October 1982. The unit has not been able to completely relinquish the colorful markings of old. (Douglas R Tachauer)

Grumman F-14A Tomcat of VF-143 at NAS Oceana, VA in October of 1982. (Douglas R Tachauer)

Douglas TA-4J Skyhawk of VC-12, NAS Oceana, VA, October 1982. No attempt has been made to 'Lo-viz' this Skyhawk. (Douglas R Tachauer)

Tactically painted McDonnell F-4S of VMFA-451, NAS Oceana, VA, October 1982. (Douglas R Tachauer)

Marine A-4F Skyhawk of VMA-133, NAS Oceana, VA, October 1982. Scheme is completely 'low-Viz' except for the Black tail codes and squadron designator on the avionics hump. (Douglas R Tachauer)

Douglas A-4F Skyhawk of VA-127, October 1982 in an unusual Brown and Green scheme with 'Low-Viz' markings. (Jerry Kishpaugh)

Douglas TA-4F Skyhawk of H&MS-13, March 1983. (Peter Bergagnini)

Douglas A-4M Skyhawk of VMA-214 'The Blackhseep' at MCAS El Toro, California, April of 1983. A Black ram with White horns is painted just behind the air intake. (Douglas R Tachauer)

Vought A-7B Corsair II of VA-304, NAS Alameda, California, April 1983. (Douglas R Tachauer)

(Below) Grumman E-1B Tracer (WF-2) of VAW-11, WHISKEY detachment, being trapped aboard KITTY HAWK (CVA-63) on 22 October 1962. The E-1B Tracer was designated WF-2 Tracer prior to September 1962. At the time of this photograph the fuselage designator, WF-2, had not yet been changed. Color scheme is the standard Light Gull Gray over Glossy Insignia White. (USN via Harry Gann)

(Below) NAS Willow Grove, Pennsylvania Beech UH-45J in 'Hi-Viz' scheme, mid-1960s. (Eric Lundahl via Harry Gann)

(Below) Sikorsky HH-52A SeaKing in August of 1963 carrying out a basket hoist rescue drill at the USCG Air Station, Brooklyn, New York. This HH-52A was still painted in the 'Hi-Viz' scheme of Fluorescent Blaze Orange/Insignia White when most other USCG aircraft were using International Orange in place of the Fluorescent Blaze Orange paint. (USCG via T E Doll)

(Below) North American T-28B/D at China Lake, California during 1961 in Target Drone Director colors of Engine Gray fuselage, Orange Yellow wings and Fluorescent Red Orange tail and wing stripes. This scheme was directed by MIL-C-18263Bs(Wep), Amendment 2 of 7 December 1959. Exhaust panel on the side of the aircraft is Black as is the front of engine cowling. (B R Jackson)

(Above) Grumman HU-16E Albatross flying out of USCG Air Station at Biloxi, Mississippi in 1964. The Coast Guard Albatross was formerly designated UF-2G. (USCG via T E Doll)

(Below) Number Six Blue Angels Grumman F11F-1 Tiger during 1962. Pilot at this time was Lt Dan MacIntyre. (Harry Gann)

(Above) T-28B Trojan attached to NAS North Island, California in November of 1964. Fluorescent Red Orange and Insignia White scheme with station name and other markings in Black. (T E Doll)

F3H-2 Demon (145226) of VF-31 off SARATOGA at NAS Cecil Field, Fla in October of 1962. Trim color is Insignia Red. Felix the Cat emblem is in a White circle in the center of the Red chevron, behind the squadron emblem is an E for Excellence. (USN)

Douglas TA-4F of VA-127, in a Tan and Dark Green scheme with Medium Gray lettering, June 1983. (Jerry Kishpaugh)

Vought A-7E Corsair II of VA-25, June 1983. (Jerry Kishpaugh)

Northrop 'TOP GUN' F5E Tiger in Tan and Green paint. May 1983. (Jerry Kishpaugh)

North American OV-10A Bronco of VMO-1 in overall Dark Green on 16 July 1983. (Douglas R Tachauer)

Grumman EA-6A Prowler of VAQ-209, 22 July 1983. (Douglas R Tachauer)

Northrop F-18A Hornets of VMFA-531, at MCAS El Toro, California. October 1983. (Douglas R Tachauer)

McDonnell RF-4B of VMFP-3 at MCAS El Toro, California, October 1983. This Phantom II has had the White undersurfaces removed leaving overall Light Gull Gray. Most of the early 'High-Viz' markings remain unchanged. (Douglas R Tachauer)

Douglas A-4M Skyhawk of VMA-223, 20 June 1984. This is an excellent example of the tactical Gray color scheme with 'low Viz' markings. (Douglas R Tachauer)

Douglas TA-4F of the H&MS-31 '31st Aggressors', June 1984. Just behind the engine intake warning chevron is an eagle with the wording "31 AGGRESSORS" below it. (Douglas R Tachauer)

Douglas A-4M Skyhawk of the Naval Air Test Center Strike Aircraft Test Program, June 1984. This aircraft, the last production A-4 (160264), while it carries a tactical scheme and Low-Viz markings, the squadron has not given up its Red Trim. (Douglas R Tachauer)

Grumman F9F-8T Cougar trainer of VA-127 at NAS North Island in November 1964. VA-127 was part of Replacement Air Group 12 and as such, trained pilots for duty with the Fleet. Fluorescent Red Orange and Insignia White scheme. (T E Doll)

Douglas A-4B Skyhawk of VMA-214, Detachment N, flying from HORNET (CVS-12). HORNET was then part of Anti-submarine Air Group 57. Trim colors on this VMA-214 'Blacksheep' Skyhawk are appropriately Black. NAS North Island during 1964. (Clay Jansson)

(Above) McDonnell F3B Demon of VF-161 off ORISKANY (CVA-34) at NAS Miramar, California in 1964. Trim color is Insignia Red identifying the first squadron of the Air Group. Scheme is the standard Light Gull Gray over Insignia White. (Harry Gann)

(Below) Lockheed's SP-2H Neptune in the Light Gull Gray over Insignia White scheme designated for VP aircraft in MIL-C-18263D(Wep) issued on 29 June 1964. VP-18 trim colors were Black and Orange Yellow. (Eric Lundahl via Harry Gann)

HUP-2 with an Insignia White solar reflecting top over Glossy Engine Gray undersides, 1965. (USN via William T Larkins)

In May of 1964 VF-13 completed the last cruise for East Coast based F3B Demons on board SHANGRI LA (CVA-38). 'Fighting Thirteen' had received their Demons in September 1962 after being the last squadron to fly the F6A (F4D-1). The Demon's trim color is Insignia Red. (VFP-62 via W A Riley)

(Below) Lockheed T-1A (144199) attached to NAS Twin Cities, Minnesota. Overall Aircraft Gray scheme appeared on many Reserve aircraft, but does not appear in official documents. The order covering this scheme for Reserve aircraft most likely originated from the office of the Chief of Naval Air Reserve Training. All codes are Black on this T-1A. 1965/66. (Eric Lundahl via Harry Gann)

Grumman A6A Intruders of Attack Squadron 42 (VA-42), the first Intruder squadron in the United States Navy. VA-42 was a component of Combat Readiness Replacement Air Group 4 headquartered at NAS Cecil Field, Florida. VA-42, operating out of NAS Oceana, Va, trained future A6 units for Fleet duty. The 'Green Pawns' of VA-42, were carrier qualified on FORRESTAL (CVA-59) on 24 August 1963, with Lt W A Caldwell making the first squadron A6 trap. Tail trim color of VA-42 Intruders is Light Green signifying fifth squadron. (USN via W A Riley)

THE VIETNAM WAR

On 2 August 1964, USS MADDOX and USS TURNER JOY were attacked by torpedo boats while patrolling International waters in the Gulf of Tonkin off the coast of Vietnam. On 5 August, the President of the United States, Lyndon B Johnson, ordered the United States Navy to take offensive action against the North Vietnamese. Two US carriers, CONSTELLATION and TICONDEROGA carried out retaliatory strikes along the North Vietnam coast.

The United States was soon involved in a brush fire war that would build to become a major American effort and see some very unusual color schemes incorporated. From this date on, and until the end of the Vietnam war, United States Navy and Marine Corps aircraft would appear in a number of various camouflage patterns. Very surprising is the fact that there is no official documentation that we (the authors) have been able to locate, delineating these paint schemes. The paint schemes seem to have been administered to various aircraft on the basis of either a verbal order or a written request that has since been destroyed. The only documentation that could possibly cover these unusual paint schemes was found in **MIL-C-18263C(Wep)** of 27 December 1961.

Under **MIL-C-18263C** in the section governing application of removable paint, it was stated that temporary paint could be applied over the permanent paint finish by field activities when authorized by the applicable command. The use of a permanent paint finish for obtaining the prescribed color configuration was not advisable in certain cases. Two of these *certain cases* were listed as addition of temporary markings and seasonal color schemes, and obliteration of temporary markings for special missions. These two cases would hold true for two instances that can be substantiated by photographic evidence aboard USS CONSTELLATION and USS KITTY HAWK while operating in the South China Sea off the coast of Vietnam during 1966.

CONSTELLATION'S VA-65 A-6A Intruders were painted Non-Specular Dark Green (34079), and Non-Specular Olive Drab (34102) on the top surfaces. Under surfaces remained Glossy Insignia White (17875).

KITTY HAWK'S VA-85 A-6As used a solid top color of Non-Specular Dark Green (34079). The under surfaces remained Glossy Insignia White. The RA-5C Vigilantes of KITTY HAWK's RVAH-13 wore top surface colors of Non-Specular Dark Green (34079), Non-Specular Olive Drab (34102) and Non-Specular Tan (30219). Under surfaces remained Glossy Insignia White. RVAH-6 on CONSTELLATION omitted the Tan color from their RA-5Cs and used only the Dark Green and Olive Drab. This was the only time that this paint scheme appeared on US Navy aircraft operating from carriers and was never used again. Through one unofficial source, it was stated that the colors used were of a water based paint and removed after a very short time (before completion of the cruise).

(Below) Douglas A-1H Skyraider in temporary camouflage scheme used during one Vietnam cruise in which KITTY HAWK (CVA-63) and CONSTELLATION (CVA-64) took part. This camouflage experiment, in 1966, did not meet with much approval and was abandoned at the completion of the cruise. Top color on this A-1H is Medium Green (34079), undersides are standard Insignia White. (Douglas)

TOP GUN

A few Douglas A4 Skyhawks began to appear on West Coast Naval air stations in a three tone camouflage of Brown, Tan and Green. These aircraft were used as *aggressors* in war game exercises.

Top Gun — The paint schemes applied to these aircraft were designed for a specific purpose, to represent the enemy. They changed from time to time both in color and design, depending on the need and were finished according to the wishes of the local commander.

MIL-I-18464E(Wep) of 20 May 1964 was twice amended; once on 24 August 1964, and again on 16 December 1965. The first amendment had no real significance as to changes for the actual markings and marking locations for Navy or Marine Corps aircraft. The major change was the substitution of a revised list of aircraft designation changes that had occurred in September 1962.

(Above) Field Green CH-46As during operations in South Vietnam. A welcome sight to tired Marines. The CH-46 "brought 'em in and brought 'em home". These two are on one of the many reconnaissance patrols behind enemy lines in the Dong Ha area during April of 1966 and are recalled by former Marine Corps Corporal Randy L Robb, "The pilots often flew us in under the harshest of conditions but they really topped themselves when it came to getting us out. Sometimes a pick-up point was under fire but they still made it in to get us and I'll never forget that." (USMC via Randy L Robb)

(Above) Douglas KA-3B of VAH-4 in a Medium Green (34079) temporary camouflage scheme used for a short time in 1966. VAH-4 was assigned the tail code "ZB" not visible in this photo. (Hideki Yamauchi)

(Above) Freshly painted RA-5C Vigilante of RVAH-6 in Medium Green (34079) and Olive Drab (34102) upper surfaces on 28 April 1966 at NAS North Island, California prior to the Vietnam cruise of CONSTELLATION (CVA-64). (Clay Jansson via The Hook)

(Right) RA-5C Vigilantes of RVAH-13 from KITTY HAWK (CVA-63) carried a three color experimental camouflage of Medium Green (34079), Olive Drab (34102) and Tan (30219). RVAH-6 from CONSTELLATION omitted the Tan from their RA-5C's, using only the green shades. (USN)

NEW AIRCRAFT DESIGNATIONS 18 Sep 1962

ATTACK SERIES

CURRENT	FORMER
A-1E	AD-5
EA-1E	AD-5W
EA-1F	AD-5Q
A-1G	AD-5N
A-1H	AD-6
A-1J	AD-7
A-2A	AJ-1
YA-3A	Y/A3D-1
A-3A	A3D-1
YEA-3A	Y/A3D-1Q
EA-3A	A3D-1Q
YRA-3A	Y/A3D-1P
A-3B	A3D-1
EA-3B	A3D-2Q
YRA-3B	Y/A3D-2P
RA-3B	A3D-2P
TA-3B	A3D-2T
YA-4A	Y/A4D-1
A-4A	A-4D-1
YA-4B	Y/A4D-2
A-4B	A4D-2
YA-4C	Y/A4D-2N
A-4C	A4D-2N
A-4E	A4D-5
YA-5	Y/A3J-1
A-5A	A3J-1
A-5B	A3J-2
RA-5C	A3J-3
EA-6A	A2F-1H

BOMBER SERIES

CURRENT	FORMER
UB-16J	JD-1
DB-26J	JD-1D

CARGO/TRANSPORT SERIES

CURRENT	FORMER
C-140C	UV-1
RC-45J	SNB-5P
TC-45J	SNB-5
C-47H	R4D-5
EC-47H	R4D-5Q
LC-47H	R4D-5L
SC-47H	R4D-5S
TC-47H	R4D-5R
VC-47H	R4D-5Z
C-47J	R4D-6
EC-47J	R4D-6Q
LC-47J	R4D-6L
SC-47J	R4D-6S
TC-47J	R4D-6R
VC-47J	R4D-6Z
TC-47K	R4D-7
VC-54N	R5D-1Z
C-54P	R5D-2
VC-54P	R5D-2Z
C-54Q	R5D-3
VC-54Q	R5D-3Z
C-54R	R5D-4R
C-54S	R5D-5
VC-54S	R5D-5Z
C-54T	R5D-5R
C-117D	R4D-8
LC-117D	R4D-8L
VC-117D	R4D-8Z
C-118B	R6D-1
VC-118B	R6D-1Z
C-119F	R4Q-2
C-121-J	R7V-1
EC-121K	WV-2
YEC-121K	Y/WV-2
EC-121L	WV-2E
EC-121M	WV-2Q
TC-117D	R4D-8T
C-130F	GV-1U
KC-130F	GV-1
LC-130F	C-130BL
C-130G	C-130E
C-131F	R4Y-1
C-131G	R4Y-2
F-8D	F8U-2N
C-1A	TF-1
EC-1A	TF-1Q
C-2A	NEW(COD)

SPECIAL ELECTRONIC INSTALLATION

CURRENT	FORMER
E-1B	WF-2
E2A	W2F-1

FIGHTER SERIES

CURRENT	FORMER
F-111B	TFX
F-1C	FJ-3
DF-1C	FJ-3D
MF-1C	FJ-3M
DF-1D	FJ-3D2
YF-1E	Y/FJ-4
F-1E	FJ-4
YAF-1E	YFJ-4B
AF-1E	FJ-4B
F-2C	F2H-3
F-2D	F2H-4
YF-3B	Y/F3H-2
F-3B	F3H-2
MF-3B	F3H-2M
F-3C	F3H-2N
F-4A	F4H-1F
F-4B	F4H-1
RF-4B	F4H-1P
F-6A	Y/F4D-1
F-6A	F4D-1
DF-6A	F4D-1
YF-7A	Y/F2Y-1
YF-8A	Y/F8U-1
DF-8A	F8U-1D
QF-8A	F8U-1KD
YRF-8A	Y/F8U-1P
RF-8A	F8U-1P
TF-8A	F8U-1T
F-8B	F8U-1E
YF-8C	Y/F8U-2
F-8C	F8U-2
YF-8D	Y/F8U-2N
YF-8E	Y/F8U-2NE
F-8E	F-8U-2NE
DF-8F	F8U-1
DF-9E	F9F-5KD
F-9F	F9F-6
DF-9F	F9F-6D

SPECIAL ELECTRONIC INSTALLATION

CURRENT	FORMER
QF-9F	F9F-6K
QF-9G	F9F-6K2
F-9H	F9F-7
F-9J	F9F-8
YAF-9J	Y/F9F-8B
AF-9J	F9F-8B
YTF-9J	Y/F9F-8T
TF-9J	F9F-8T
RF-9J	F9F-8P
F-10A	F3D-1
F-10B	F3D-2
F-10B	F3D-2Q
MF-10B	F3D-2M
TF-10B	SF3D-2T2
YF-11A	Y/F11F-1
F-11A	F11F-1

HELICOPTER SERIES

CURRENT	FORMER
UH-1E	HU-1E
UH-2A	HU2K-1
UH-2B	HU2K-1U
YSH-3A	Y/HSS-2
SH-3A	HSS-2
VH-3A	HSS-2Z
TH-13L	HTL-4
TH-13M	HTL-6
TH-13N	HTL-7
UH-13P	HUL-1
HH-13Q	HUL-1G
UH-13R	HUL-1M
CH-19E	HRS-3
UH-19F	H04S-3
HH-19G	HO4S-3G
UH-25B	HUP-2
UH-25C	HUP-3
LH-34D	HUS-1L
YSH-34G	Y/HSS-1
SH-34G	HSS-1
UH-34D	HUS-1
VH-34D	HUS-1Z
UH-34E	HUS-1A
HH-34F	HUS-1G
SH-34H	HSS-1F
YSH-34J	Y/HSS-1N
SH-34J	HSS-1N
CH-37C	HR2S-1
UH-43C	HUK-1
OH-43D	HOK-1
TH-43E	HTK-1
CH-46A	HRB-1
QH-50A	DSN-1
QH-50B	DSN-2
QM-50C	DSN-3
XH-51A	NEW(Rigid Rotor)
	T-2A

OBSERVATION SERIES

CURRENT	FORMER
O-1B	OE-1
OC-1C	OE-2

PATROL SERIES

CURRENT	FORMER
P-2D	P2V-4
P-2E	P2V-5F
DP-2E	P2V-5FD
EP-2E	P2V-5FE
SP-2E	P2V-5FS
P-2F	P2V-6
MP-2F	P2V-6M
TP-2F	P2V-6T
P-2G	P2V-6F
YP-2H	Y/P2V-7
P-2H	P2V-7
SP-2H	P2V-7S
LP-2J	P2V-7LP
YP-3A	Y/P3V-1
P-3A	P3V-1
QP-4B	P4Y-2K
P-5A	P5M-1
SP-5A	P5M-1S
TP-5A	P5M-1T
P5B	P5M-2
SP-5B	P5M-2S

ANTI-SUB SERIES

CURRENT	FORMER
S-2A	S2F-1
YS-2A	Y/S2F-1
TS-2A	S2F-1T
S-2B	S2F-1S
S-2C	S2F-2
RS-2C	S2F-2P
US-2C	S2F-2
S-2D	S2F-3
S-2E	S2F-3S

TRAINER SERIES

CURRENT	FORMER
T-1A	T2V-1
YT-2A	YT2J-1
T2J-1	T2J-2
T2B	SAME
T-28A	SAME
T-28B	T-28BD
DT-28D	SAME
T-28C	TV-2
T-33B	TV-2D
DT-33B	TV-2KD
DT-33C	T-34B
T-34B	Y/T-34B
YT-34B	T3J-1
T-39D	

UTILITY SERIES

CURRENT	FORMER
U-1B	UC-1
U-S6A	L-20A
U-11A	UQ-1
HU-16C	UF-1
LU-16C	UF-1L
TU-16C	UF-1T
HU-16D	UF-2
HU-16E	UF-2G

VERTICAL TAKE-OFF SERIES

CURRENT	FORMER
X-22A	VTOL

AIRSHIP SERIES

CURRENT	FORMER
EZ-1B	ZPG-2W
SZ-1B	ZPG-2
EZ-1C	ZPG-3W

MIL-I-18464E(Wep) AMENDMENT 2 16 December 1964

The first two changes incorporated in this amendment were that all parts markings would now be in accordance with **MIL-M-25047** and markings for Emergency Escape Systems were now covered under **MIL-A-25165**.

Added to **MIL-I-18464E** by **Amendment No. 2** was a new section covering production block markings. Contractor production control blocks were to be designated by applying a lower case letter on the fuselage immediately following the aircraft serial number using the letter 'a' for the first block. Consecutive changes shall be designated in order by the letters 'b' through 'z'. If additional change markings were required the following double letter series shall be applied: 'aa', 'ab', through 'az'; 'ba' through 'bc'.

The production block designation was mandatory, and size and location were as follows: on the fuselage, immediately following the aircraft serial number, size of the letters was to be one-half the height of the serial number.

PATROL AIRCRAFT

Patrol aircraft that were at present finished in the Light Gull Gray color on the undersurface, **MIL-C-18263D,** now carried the Branch of Service marking and unit identifying letters and numerals on the undersurface of the left wing. Color of these letters and numerals were to be in Low Gloss White and the national insignia was to be in low gloss colors.

MIL-C-18263E(Wep) 11 May 1965

On 11 May 1965, a new document governing the exterior colors of Naval aircraft was issued. This specification, **MIL-C-18263E(Wep),** created the largest change in color schemes to Naval aircraft in the last eight years, by the elimination of Semi-Gloss Fluorescent Red-Orange from almost all aircraft that had used it in the past, and replacing it with Glossy International Orange.

HIGH VISIBILITY COLOR CONFIGURATIONS

The high visibility color configurations were employed on aircraft in the Training Command, excluding Reserve Training, target control and SAR aircraft, target and drones. The color, Glossy International Orange, was standard for all high visibility applications, except for targets and drones. These remained in the Semi-Gloss Fluorescent Red-Orange.

All helicopters, such as the TH, UH-25B and UH-19F, used for training were painted overall Glossy International Orange. Helicopters such as the CH-19E, UH-25 and UH-2, assigned to search and rescue were also painted in a Glossy International Orange paint scheme, replacing the portions that had previously been Semi-Gloss Fluorescent Red-Orange.

The general configurations of all high visibility markings for all aircraft remained the same; only the color was changed.

BASIC COLOR SCHEMES OF MIL-C-18263E(Wep)

ATTACK (VA)	NS	LIGHT GULL GRAY
	G	INSIGNIA WHITE
FIGHTER	NS	LIGHT GULL GRAY
	G	INSIGNIA WHITE
MARINE OBSERVATION (VO)	NS	FIELD GREEN
PATROL (VP)	NS	LIGHT GULL GRAY
	G	INSIGNIA WHITE
TRANSPORTS (VR)		
LANDPLANES	G	AIRCRAFT GRAY
	G	INSIGNIA WHITE
SEAPLANES	SG	SEAPLANE GRAY
TRAINER (VT)-LANDPLANE		
SINGLE RECIPROCATING	G	INSIGNIA WHITE
ENGINE	G	INTERNATIONAL ORANGE
MULTI-RECIPROCATING	G	INSIGNIA WHITE
ENGINE	G	INTERNATIONAL ORANGE
TRAINER (VT)-SEAPLANE		
ADVANCED AND		
PRIMARY	SG	SEAPLANE GRAY
	G	INTERNATIONAL ORANGE
TRAINER (VT)-JET		
INTERMEDIATE	G	INSIGNIA WHITE
BASIC	G	INTERNATIONAL ORANGE
PRIMARY		
TARGET TOWING (VU)	G	ORANGE YELLOW
	G	ENGINE GRAY
	G	INTERNATIONAL ORANGE
UTILITY LANDPLANES (VU)	G	INSIGNIA WHITE
	G	AIRCRAFT GRAY
UTILITY SEAPLANES (VU)	G	INSIGNIA WHITE
	G	SEAPLANE GRAY
SEARCH AND RESCUE		
SEAPLANES (VS)	G	INSIGNIA WHITE
	SG	SEAPLANE GRAY
	G	INTERNATIONAL ORANGE
WARNING(VW)-LANDBASED		
WITH NORMAL OPERATING		
ALTITUDES	G	AIRCRAFT GRAY
GREATER THAN 15,000 FEET	G	INSIGNIA WHITE
WARNING(VW)-LANDBASED		
WITH NORMAL OPERATING		
ALTITUDES		
GREATER THAN 15,000 FEET	SG	SEAPLANE GRAY
WARNING(VW)-CARRIER		
BASED	NS	LIGHT GULL GRAY
	G	INSIGNIA WHITE
HELICOPTERS		
UTILITY (HU)	G	ENGINE GRAY
CARGO UNLOADING(HC)	G	ENGINE GRAY
OBSERVATION (HO)	G	ENGINE GRAY
TRANSPORT (HR)	G	ENGINE GRAY
SUBMARINE SEARCH		
AND ATTACK (HT)	G	ENGINE GRAY
TRAINER (HT)	G	INTERNATIONAL ORANGE
TARGET (KD)	G	INSIGNIA WHITE
	SG	FLUORESCENT YELLOW-ORANGE
	G	INSIGNIA RED
TARGET DRONE (DK)	SG	FLUORESCENT YELLOW-ORANGE
DRONE CONTROL (KD)	G	ORANGE YELLOW
	G	INTERNATIONAL ORANGE
	G	ENGINE GRAY
DRONE, ANTI-SUBMARINE	G	ENGINE GRAY
	SG	FLUORESCENT RED ORANGE
	SG	FLUORESCENT GREEN
AIRSHIPS (ALL TYPES)		ALUMINUM
	NS	LIGHT GULL GRAY

G = Glossy SG = Semi-Gloss NS = Non-Specular

On 1 July 1965, Fleet Air Wing 8 was commissioned at Naval Air Station, Moffett Field, and all Helicopter Utility Squadrons (HU) were redesignated Helicopter Combat Support Squadrons (HC) and Utility Squadrons (VU) were redesignated Fleet Composite Squadrons (VC) to bring their designations more in line with their functions and composition.

(Left) F8U-2N Crusader carries the contractor's production control block number (lower case 'e' adjacent to aircraft BuNo, 148645e). (VFP-63)

Beech TC-45J from NAS Los Alamitos, California during the mid-1960s. Insignia White over Light Gull Gray color scheme. (Eric Lundahl viaHarry Gann)

(Below) Grumman EA-6A Intruder of VMCJ-2 in standard Gray over White color scheme, 1966. Insignia on rudder is Black as are all other markings. (USMC via William T. Larkins)

Sikorsky SH-34J from GUAM (LPH-9) in overall Glossy Engine Gray with Insignia White codes. Tail boom warning stripe is Orange Yellow. GUADALCANAL (LPH-7) is in the background. Mid-1960s. (USN via Jerry Kishpaugh)

(Below) Boeing-Vertol CH-46A of HHM-161 in South Vietnam, during the mid-1960s. Taking over from the UH-34D, the CH-46A became the mainstay of Marine Corps Search and Destroy missions in Vietnam. Marines literally jumped to the ground from these CH-46s in operations such as OPERATION BUFFALO II in December of 1966 at Qua Viet, DMZ, and OPERATION HICKORY I in the Mekong Delta during January of 1966. This CH-46 with its well worn Field Green paint and Black lettering was typical of Vietnam. (USMC via Randy L Robb)

MIL-I-18464F(Wep) 12 July 1965

This document, issued on 12 July 1965, was much the same as **MIL-I-18464E(Wep)** of 20 May 1964. The two amendments followingthe previous specification had been incorporated into **MIL-I-18464F** and only two major changes were introduced.

RESERVE AIRCRAFT MARKINGS

The first major change of this specification was that the Orange band on the fuselage of Reserve aircraft was no longer required, and that the station name would be an optional marking for all Navy and Marine Corps Reserve aircraft.

SQUADRON DESIGNATION WITHIN CARRIER AIR GROUPS

A seventh squadron color for Air Group squadron designations was added; Glossy Insignia Blue. The breakdown now read as follows:

1st Squadron or Unit	Glossy Insignia Red
2nd Squadron or Unit	Glossy Orange Yellow
3rd Squadron or Unit	Glossy Light Blue
4th Squadron or Unit	Glossy International Orange
5th Squadron or Unit	Glossy Light Green
6th Squadron or Unit	Glossy Black
7th Squadron or Unit	Glossy Insignia Blue

Location of these markings were the same as in previous specification, propeller spinner(s) and approximately the top 7 inches of the vertical tail surface(s), on both sides above the Unit Identifying Letters.

With the addition of the seventh squadron color, all aircraft with a designation of VAW, VFP, VA(AW), etc., were deleted. However, the Maroon marking remained for other squadrons.

MIL-C-18263E(AS) AMENDMENT 1 26 July 1967

This amendment to **MIL-C-18263E** incorporated several changes in the color schemes of Navy and Marine Corps aircraft.

The first change deleted the Reserve aircraft from the Special markings section. This was due to the deletion of the Orange band mentioned under **MIL-I-18464F**.

SOLAR HEAT REFLECTIONS

All aircraft formally known as Zulu aircraft were now signified as aircraft used in a VIP or staff capacity, now were to carry a Black stripe below the white area of the solar heat reflecting roof, and a Black chevron on the nacelles for decorative purposes.

WALKWAYS AND STEPS

Carrier aircraft walkways which were painted NS Light Gull Gray remained so, unless a situation of gross contamination was prevalent, due to the aircraft configuration; the walkways were then painted NS Dark Gull Gray.

Several changes in the overall color scheme of aircraft were also introduced in this amendment.

The OV-10 Bronco, the Marine Corps' newest observation airplane was painted NS Field Green on the upper surface, and NS Light Gull Gray on the bottom surface. Normally, Marine observation aircraft were painted overall NS Field Green.

Warning aircraft, landbased with normal operating altitudes of 15,000 feet or less were now painted Semi-Gloss Seaplane Gray and Glossy Insignia White; solar reflecting roof.

SH-3 helicopters used in the capacity of anti-submarine and search were painted Glossy Insignia White on the upper surfaces down to an undulating line extending from the bottom of the lower window in the pilot's compartment to the bottom of the tail hinge, and the lower portion was painted NS Light Gull Gray.

MIL-I-18464F(AS)* AMENDMENT 1 23 February 1967

With this amendment, the markings for helicopters were altered slightly in the application of the words ABANDON CHUTE. This marking, applied to all Search and Rescue helicopters, could now be applied to other helicopters engaged in search and rescue work at the discretion of the cognizant commands in an appropriate location so as to be readily visible from below.

NAVAL ATTACHE (ALUSNA) AIRCRAFT MARKINGS

The markings for NAVAL ATTACHE aircraft would now apply to NAVAL MISSION aircraft; either a NAVAL ATTACHE marking or a NAVAL MISSION marking was to be applied as applicable.

The AS replacing the WEP following the specification number was not officially rendered until* **Amendment 2; however, it appears on the specification number of **Amendment 1.**

MIL-I-18464F(AS) AMENDMENT 2 11 March 1968

By this amendment, basic specification **MIL-I-18464F(Wep)** was changed to read **MIL-I-18464F(AS)**, and through the specification, Bureau of Naval Weapons was changed to read Naval Air Systems Command.

NAVAL ATTACHE (ALUSNA) AIRCRAFT MARKINGS

The American flag, for ALUSNA aircraft was now located on the vertical tail surface in such a position that it was horizontal, and the union was in the uppermost on both sides of the vertical surfaces. On aircraft having multiple vertical tail surfaces, the flag appeared only on the outboard sides. The flag on the left side and right side of the aircraft was applied with the Blue field forward and the stripes extending aft. The bars of the flag were to appear to be trailing at all times, and the flag was to be located symmetrically on all surfaces.

On 1 July 1968, the Naval Air Reserve was reorganized into wings and squadrons known collectively as the Naval Air Reserve Force and, effective 1 August, Commander Naval Air Reserve Training assumed additional duty as Commander Naval Air Reserve Force. This change was made to insure a more rapid and efficient transition to combat status in the event of mobilization.

On 1 April 1970, two Reserve Carrier Air Wings, CVWR-20 and CVWR-30 were commissioned, followed by CVSGR-70 and CVSGR-80 on 1 May. This was a continuation of the program initiated in July 1968 mentioned above. The reorganization placed all carrier-type squadrons in two reserve carrier wings and two carrier ASW groups. Twelve VP and three VR squadrons joined the carrier squadrons under the control of Commander Naval Air Reserve Force.

MIL-C-18263F(AS) 29 June 1971

With the issuing of this latest painting specification covering the exterior of Naval aircraft, a great many color changes were inaugurated. Minor changes in the basic structure of the specification were also evident.

The first major change was the deletion of the use of removable paint for temporary paint schemes. This section had been carried throughout all of the previous documents, but would no longer be used by Naval or Marine Corps aircraft. In the case of the temporary paint scheme for Arctic operations, the White solar reflecting roof being painted with removable Glossy Engine Gray was no longer used. These aircraft were now painted with a permanent Glossy Engine Gray roof. Temporary use of the High Visibility paint scheme for aircraft operating in high density areas was also deleted.

SEARCH AND RESCUE SCHEME

SAR Helicopters, except when configured for combat operations, were now finished in a high visibility color scheme of Glossy International Orange and Glossy Engine Gray.

PROPELLER ASSEMBLIES

Propeller assemblies and helicopter blades, main and tail rotor, were now covered under **MIL-F-18264**. Color and markings remained the same as **MIL-C-18263E**.

ENGINE COWLING INTERIORS

The interior of engine cowlings were now painted Glossy Light Gray.

Project Trim (Trail Interdiction Mission) Lockheed AP-2H Neptune modified for Project Trim in 1967. The AP-2H was modified from a standard SP-2H Neptune with the MAD boom being removed and an Aero 11/A tail turret installed in its place. The Aero turret featured twin M-3 20MM guns. The MK-8 rocket/gunsight and infra-red Starlight scope was also carried on the AP-2H. This Neptune also carried eight 40MM Honeywell grenade launchers in the bomb bay.

Project Trim Lockheed AP-2H banks away showing underside of the aircraft and its wrap-a-round camouflage scheme. Carried on the wings on the outboard stations were either two low drag general purpose MK-82 500 lb. bombs and one MK-81 250 lb. bomb, or two MK-77 napalm bombs on each wing. Fiberglass props were driven by the Wright R-3350 engines. Starting out as Project Trim, the unit was redesignated VAH-21 in December of 1968. Home base was Sangley Point, Republic of the Philippines but most of its flying was done in the Mekong Delta region of South Vietnam, flying out of Camranh Bay. VAH-21 flew most of their missions at night. Co-author Doll worked on all four AP-2Hs of Project Trim in 1967. (Lockheed)

(Below) The Lockheed AP-2H featured a three Gray color scheme, Light Gull Gray (36440), Dark Gull Gray (36231) and Sea Gray (36118), all non-specular. Small 12 inch US national insignias were placed on fuselage sides but not on wings. The wings incorporated 7.62mm mini-guns mounted in a pod firing 6,000 rounds per minute. The pylons on which the mini-guns were mounted were angled at approximately 30 degrees down and boresighted to converge approximately 500 feet ahead of the airplane. (Lockheed)

BASIC COLOR SCHEMES MIL-C-18263F(AS)

Carrier Based Attack (VA)	Glossy Light Gray Glossy Insignia White
Carrier Based Fighter (VF)	Glossy Light Gray Glossy Insignia White
Marine Observation (VO)	Non-Specular Field Green*
Patrol (VP)	Glossy Light Gray Glossy Insignia White
Transports (VR)	
Landplanes	Glossy Light Gray Glossy Insignia White
Trainer (VT)	Glossy Insignia White Glossy International Orange
Seaplanes	Glossy Engine Gray Glossy International Orange
Utility (VU)	
Landplanes	Glossy Insignia White Glossy Light Gray
Seaplanes	Glossy Insignia White Glossy Engine Gray
Search and Rescue Seaplanes	Glossy Insignia White Glossy Engine Gray Glossy International Orange
Warning (VW) Landbased with normal operating altitudes greater than 15,000 feet	Glossy Light Gray Glossy Insignia White
Landbased with normal operating altitudes of 15,000 feet or less	Glossy Engine Gray Glossy Insignia White
Carrier-based VW	Glossy Light Gray Glossy Insignia White
Target Towing and Drone	Glossy Light Gray Glossy Insignia White Glossy International Orange
Target (KD)	Glossy Insignia White Glossy Fluorescent Yellow Orange
Target Drone (DS)	Semi-gloss Fluorescent Yellow Orange
Helicopters	
Utility (HU)	Glossy Engine Gray
Cargo Unloading (HC)	Glossy Engine Gray
Observation (HO)	Glossy Engine Gray
Transport (HR)	Glossy Engine Gray
Submarine Search and Attack (HS) except SH-3	Glossy Engine Gray
Trainer (HT)	Glossy Insignia White Glossy International Orange
Drone — Anti-Submarine	Glossy Engine Gray Semi-Gloss Fluorescent Semi-Gloss Fluorescent Green

**Except Marine OV-10 aircraft which were to be painted Glossy Light Gray on the bottom surfaces and Non-Specular Insignia White on the top surfaces of the wings. The balance of the OV-10 was painted Non-Specular Field Green.*

All changes in the basic color scheme, from **MIL-C-18263E(Wep)** of 11 May 1965 were marked with an asterisk. The changes in the attack, fighter, patrol and carrier based aircraft were in the colors only, Light Gull Gray was changed to Light Gray. Application remained the same as previously outlined.

As of 1 July 1971, the assignment of identification letters for Navy and Marine Corps aircraft was as follows:

NAVAL AIRCRAFT UNITS

ATTACK CARRIER AIR WINGS

CVW-1	AB	CVW-14	NL
CVW-2	NE	CVW-17	NL
CVW-3	AC	CVW-19	NM
CVW-5	NF	CVW-21	NP
CVW-6	AE	RCVW-4*	AD
CVW-7	AG	RCVW-12**	NJ
CVW-8	AJ	CVWR-20	AF (Reserve)
CVW-9	NG	CVWR-30	ND (Reserve)
CVW-11	NH		

ASW AIR GROUPS

CVSG-53	NS	CVGS-59	NT
CVGS-54	AT	CVSR-70	AW (Reserve CVGR)
CVGS-56	AU	CVSR-80	NW (Reserve CVGR)

LIGHT ATTACK

VAL-4 UM

HELICOPTER MINE COUNTERMEASURE SQUADRON

HM-12 DH

PHOTOGRAPHIC

VFP-63 PP

TACTICAL ELECTRONIC WARFARE

VAQ-33	GD	VAQW-13	TR

CARRIER AEW

CAEWW-12	GE	VAW-111	RR
RVAW-110	TT		

AIRBORNE EARLY WARNING AND WEATHER RECONNAISSANCE

VW-4 MH

FLEET COMPOSITE

VC-1	UA	VC-6	JG
VC-2	JE	VC-7	UH
VC-3	UF	VC-8	GF
VC-5	UE	VC-10	JH

**Disestablished on 1 June 1970. RCVW-4 tail letters were retained by the following squadrons: VA-42, VA-43, VA-45, VA-174, VF-101, and VF-101 Det Oceana.*
***Disestablished on 1 June 1970. RCVW-12 tail letters were retained by the following squadrons: VF-121, VF-124, VF-126, VA-122, VA-125, VA-127 and VA-128.*

Lockheed OP-2E of Observation Squadron 67 (VO-67). These Neptunes, like those of VAH-21 (Project Trim), were extensively modified for use in Vietnam. Upper color was Medium Green (34079) over Light Gull Gray (36440). All codes are Black. The tail letters assigned were "MR". (Lockheed)

F8E Crusader of VF-211 with six North Vietnam flags painted on its ventral fin indicating the number of enemy fighters the squadron shot down in aerial combat. Trim color is Insignia Red. (LTV via B R Jackson)

PATROL

VP-1	YB	VP-26	LK
VP-4	YD	VP-30	LL
VP-5	LA	VP-31	RP
VP-6	PC	VP-40	QE
VP-8	LC	VP-44	LM
VP-11	LE	VP-45	LN
VP-16	LF	VP-46	RC
VP-17	ZE	VP-47	RD
VP-19	PE	VP-48	SF
VP-22	QA	VP-49	LF
VP-23	LF	VP-50	SG
VP-24	LR	VP-56	LQ

RECONNAISSANCE ATTACK*

RAVH-1	GH	RVAH-9	GM
RVAH-3	GJ	RVAH-12	GP
RVAH-5	GK	RVAH-13	GR
RVAH-6	GS	RVAH-14	GQ
RVAH-7	GL		

FLEET TACTICAL SUPPORT

VR-1	JK	VR-51	RV
VR-21	RZ	VR-52	JT
VR-24	JM	VRC-40	CD
VR-30	RW	VRC-50	RG
VR-50	JS		

HELICOPTER COMBAT SUPPORT

HC-1	UP	HC-5	TD
HC-2	NU	HC-6	HW
HC-3	SA	HC-7	VH
HC-4	HT		

FLEET AIR RECONNAISSANCE

VQ-1	PR	VQ-3	TC
VQ-2	WQ	VQ-4	ML

AIR TEST AND EVALUATION

VX-1	JA	VX-5	XE
VX-4	XF		

ANTARCTIC DEPLOYMENT

VXE-6 JD

OCEANOGRAPHIC DEVELOPMENT

VXN-8 JB

NAVAL AIR TRAINING NABATRACOM
(NAVAL AIR BASIC TRAINING COMMAND)

FRG	2A	NAS Pensacola
VT-1	2S	NAS Saufley Field
VT-2	2G	NAS Whiting Field
VT-3	2W	NAS Whiting Field
VT-4	2F	NAS Pensacola
VT-5	2S	NAS Saufley Field
VT-6	2P	NAS Whiting Field
VT-7	2K	NAS Meridian
VT-9	2M	NAS Meridian
VT-10	2N	NAS Pensacola
HT-8	2E	NAS Ellyson Field

NAVANTRACOM
(NAVAL AIR ADVANCED TRAINING COMMAND)

VT-21	3E	Corpus Christi
VT-22	3F	Kingsville
VT-23	3H	Kingsville
VT-24	3K	Chase Field
VT-25	3J	Chase Field
VT-26	3L	Chase Field
VT-27	3G	Corpus Christi
VT-28	3B	Corpus Christi
VT-29	3C	Corpus Christi
VT-31	3A	Corpus Christi

NATECHTRACOM
(NAVAL AIR TECHNICAL TRAINING COMMAND)

Glynco	4B	Pensacola	4P
Lakehurst	4L	Philadelphia	4P
Memphis	4M		

All other VAH squadrons show letters of parent CVW.

NARESTRACOM
(NAVAL AIR RESERVE TRAINING COMMAND)

Atlanta	7B	Willow Grove	7W
Dallas	7D	Washington	6A
Detroit	7Y	Jacksonville	6F
Glenview	7V	Alameda	6G
Los Alamitos	7L	Lakehurst	6N
New Orleans	7X	Memphis	6M
New York	7R	Norfolk	6S
So. Weymouth	7Z	North Island	

NAVY RESERVE SQUADRONS
CARRIER SQUADRONS
RESERVE LANT

	CVWR-20 TAIL CODE AF		CVWR-30 TAIL CODE ND
VF-201	Dallas	VF-301	Miramar
DVF-202	Dallas	VF-302	Miramar
VA-203	Jacksonville	VA-303	Alameda
VA-204	Memphis	VA-304	Alameda
VA-205	Detroit	VA-305	Point Mugu
VFP-206	Washington	VFP-306	Washington
VAW-207	Norfolk	VAW-307	North Island
VAQ-208	Alameda	VAQ-308	Alameda
VA-209	Glenview		
VA-210	So. Weymouth		

ANTI-SUBMARINE WARFARE

	CVSGR-70 TAIL CODE AW		**CVSGR-80 TAIL CODE NW**
VS-71	Lakehurst	VS-81	North Island
VS-72	Norfolk	VS-82	Alameda
VS-73	Lakehurst	VS-83	Whidbey Island
HS-74	Lakehurst	HS-84	Imperial Beach
HS-75	Lakehurst	HS-88	ALAMEADA
VSF-76	New Orleans	VSF-86	New Orleans
VAW-78	Norfolk	VAW-88	North Island

PATROL SQUADRONS

VP-60	LS	Glenview	VP-65	PG	Point Mugu
VP-62	LT	Jacksonville	VP-67	PL	Memphis
VP-64	LU	Willow Grove	VP-69	PJ	Whidbey Island
VP-68	LW	Patuxent River	VP-91	PM	Moffett Field
VP-90	LX	Glenview			
VP-92	LY	So. Weymouth			
VP-94	LZ	New Orleans			

TRANSPORT SQUADRONS

VR-50	Unit 1	JS	Jacksonville
VR-50	Unit 2	JS	Willow Grove
VR-51	Unit 1	RV	Alameda
VR-51	Unit 2	RV	Whidbey Island
VR-51	Unit 3	RV	Glenview
VR-52	Unit 1	JT	Dallas
VR-52	Unit 2	JT	Memphis

F-4 Phantom II of VF-11 'Red Rippers' at NAS Alameda, California in May of 1969. Trim color is Insignia Red. (Smalley via Tom Gates)

'Triple Zero' signifying the personal aircraft of the Commander Fleet Air Miramar in 1969. Pilot of this F4B is Captain Stanley W Vejtasa. Standard USN Light Gull Gray over White camouflage with Black codes. (Harry Gann)

FLEET MARINE AND MARINE SUPPORT UNITS HEADQUARTERS

HS FMFLANT	BZ	H&MS-24	EW
HS FMFPAC	WZ	H&MS-26	EL
H&MS-10	SE	H&MS-27	CZ
H&MS-11	SE	H&MS-30	SR
H&MS-12	WA	H&MS-31	EX
H&MS-13	YU	H&MS-32	DA
H&MS-14	CN	H&MS-36	WX
H&MS-15	YZ	H&MS-37	QF
H&MS-16	WW	H&MS-40	HR
H&MS-17	SZ	H&MS-56	VZ

ATTACK

VMA-211	CF	VMA-324	DX
VMA-214	WE	VMA-331	VL
VMA-223	WP	VMA-513	WF
VMA-311	WL		

FIGHTER ATTACK

VMFA-115	VE	VMFA-314	VW
VMFA-122	DC	VMFA-323	WS
VMFA-212	WD	VMFA-333	DN
VMFA-232	WT	VMFA-334	WU
VMFA-235	DB	VMFA-451	VM
VMFA-251	DW	VMFA-531	EC
VMFA-312	DR		

ALL-WEATHER ATTACK

VMA(AW)-121	VK	VMA(AW)-242	DT
VMA(AW)-224	WK	VMA(AW)-332	EA
VMA(AW)-225	CE	VMA(AW)-533	ED

OBSERVATION

VMO-1	ER	VMO-6	WB
VMO-2	VS		

AERIAL REFUELER/TRANSPORT

VMCR-152	QD	VMCR-352	QB
VMCR-252	BH		

HELICOPTER LIGHT

HML-167	TV	HML-367	VT
HML-267	UV		

HELICOPTER MEDIUM

HMM-161	YR	HMM-261	EM
HMM-162	YS	HMM-262	ET
HMM-163	YP	HMM-263	EG
HMM-164	YT	HMM-264	EH
HMM-165	YW	HMMT-302	SQ
		HMMT-402	

HELICOPTER HEAVY

HMH-361	YN	HMH-462	YF
HMH-362	YL	HMH-463	YH
HMH-363	YZ	HMHT-301	SP
HMH-461	CJ	HMHT-401	HP

HELICOPTER DEVELOPMENT

HMX-1	MX

FLEET TRAINING

VMT-103	SD	VMATAW-202	KC
VMT-203	KD	VMFAT-101	SB
VMAT-102	SC	VMFAT-201	KB

COMPOSITE RECONNAISSANCE

VMCH-1	RM	VMC-3	TN
VMC-2	CY		

HELICOPTER ATTACK

HMA-269	HF

This listing of tail codes for United States Navy and Marine Corps aircraft squadrons is the official list posted by the Chief of Naval Operations, and is not infallible. Often, the changes are not made by the involved squadron, and the office preparing the chart is not informed as to delays that might occur.

MIL-C-18263F(AS) AMENDMENT 1 9 March 1972

This amendment to **MIL-C-18263F(AS)** contained only two changes. The first was that all Marine helicopters were now painted Glossy Field Green, and the Non-Specular Insignia White on the lower surfaces of OV-10s was changed to Glossy Insignia White.

MIL-I-18464G(AS) AMENDMENT 1 14 August 1975

The main thrust of this amendment concerned the use of colors to designate the squadrons within the Carrier Air Group.

SQUADRON TYPE	ASSIGNED COLOR	FS COLOR NUMBERS
VAW	Insignia Blue	15044/35044
First VF Squadron	Insignia Red	11136/31136
Second VF Squadron	Orange-Yellow	13538/33538
First VA Squadron	Light Blue	15102/35102
Second VA Squadron	International Orange	12197/32197
Third VA Squadron	Light Green	14187/34187
RVAH/VFP	Black	17038/37038
VAQ	Maroon	10049/30049
VS Squadron	Dark Green	14062/34062
HS Squadron/HC Detachment	Magenta	17142/37142

Squadron aircraft identification colors were to conform to Federal Standard 595a. For non-camouflaged aircraft, the colors used were to be glossy finish. Camouflaged aircraft were to use lusterless colors (non-specular).

The basic color scheme applied to the exterior surface of US Naval aircraft remained the same throughout the mid-1970s. However, a new scheme for Marine Corps helicopters, H-1, H-46 and H-53, was issued during 1977.

CNO Message 121828Z issued during April of 1977 ordered a new system of low IR reflective epoxy primer coupled with a low IR reflective Field Green (34097) top coat. The new system called for a lusterless finish, the old system featured a glossy finish.

Markings were greatly reduced in size or were to be deleted entirely. If markings were applied, they were to be lusterless Black (37038).

Camouflage paint schemes have always been experimented with by the Navy. World War Two most likely represented the zenith of camouflage experimentation and national insignia change. The Vietnam war found some experimenting being carried out by CONSTELLATION and KITTY HAWK air groups during 1966. These schemes were covered earlier.

In the early 1970s, experimental schemes relative to carrier based aircraft began to gain momentum. Point Mugu's VX-4, for example, began sporting various hues on their aircraft, the most noticeable being *Vandy 1*, an all Black F-4J. This all Black scheme was first applied in 1969 to test an anti-corrosive paint system. VX-4's TA-4J and another F-4J appeared in various shades of Brown and Blue respectively. Change was in the wind...

THE FERRIS PAINT SCHEMES

In the mid-1970s, noted aviation artist, Keith Ferris, originated a deceptive paint system for experimental use on Fleet aircraft. The design featured a splinter type pattern with the colors being various shades of Gray and Blue-Gray. The US national insignia, safety and instructional markings were also varied shades of Gray.

Federal Standard color numbers 36118, 36231 and 36440 were used on some aircraft with other shades being applied to other aircraft used in the experiment. The Ferris scheme also featured the painting of a false canopy on the underside of the aircraft for added deception. The Ferris paint scheme was the design...the colors varied.

After many years of the Light Gray topside/Insignia White underside colors on naval aircraft, Mr. Ferris looked on the older scheme with amazement and asked, *why?* ...in just the right places, and, as of this writing, his designs and their impact, are still obvious.

During the final weeks of 1977, the Insignia White undersides of Navy and Marine Corps aircraft were ordered removed. Overall Light Gray became the order of the day. In 1978 the toning down of the bright squadron markings also became noticeable, with some designs being merely overpainted with shades of gray. The US national insignia also became less and less conspicuous as time moved into the 1980s.

TACTICAL PAINT SCHEMES

As the new decade began, Naval Air Systems Command was already busy finalizing the new Tactical paint scheme to be applied to Navy and Marine Corps aircraft. The new scheme was designed to minimize the initial detection range of the aircraft and reduce visual clues.

Early in the testing program, Tactical Electronic Warfare Squadron-133 (VAQ-133), using the new scheme on their EA-6B Prowler aircraft, reported good results with the new paint system. In tests conducted against the US Air Force, the Prowlers had been picked up visually as far out as thirty miles while using the old scheme of Gray over White. The new *Low-viz* scheme allowed VAQ-133 Prowlers to get within five miles of the *enemy* befor visual detection.

Gone are the heavy Black letters and numerals, and no more Red, White and Blue US national markings. More often than not, even the Red warning markings are no longer carried. And the colorful squadron markings are now only a memory.

The last word in the deadly serious game of aerial survival is SURVIVAL. While the colorful markings applied to Navy and Marine Corps aircraft were important to morale, eventually the change over will be taken in stride and a sense of camaraderie and esprit de corps will come through none the worse for wear.

TACTICAL SCHEME MARKING POLICY

General:

1. If the background color is the darkest Gray, use the Medium Gray or the marking.
2. If the background color is the Medium Gray, use the darkest Gray for the marking.
3. If the background color is the lightest Gray, use the Medium Gray for the marking.

Specific:

1. National Insignia — the star and outer bars are the background color and the rest of the insignia is the contrasting Gray color. (See general policy). The size of the national insignia will be minimum size, 12 inches.
2. Major Warning Markings — Letters/printing are in the background color and the border/background of the marking is in the contrasting Gray color. (See general policy).
3. Maintenance Markings — all maintenance markings are applied in a contrasting shade of Gray. (See general policy).

The first scheme approved under the new tactical scheme system was designed for the FA-18A Hornet. This was approved on 30 July 1980. The following is a list of model designs approved along with the dates of approval and the Federal Standard 595a color numbers to be used in the application of the Tactical paint scheme.

FA-18A	approved	30	Jul	1980	35237/36375/36495
A-4	approved	25	Aug	1980	36320/36375/36495
OA-4	approved	25	Aug	1980	36320/36375/36495
EA-6B	approved	3	Feb	1982	35237/36320/36375
F-4	approved	3	Feb	1982	35337/36320/36375
F-14	approved	3	Feb	1982	35237/36320/36375
A-6	approved	3	Feb	1982	36320/36375
A-7	approved	3	Feb	1982	36320/36375

Yet to be approved, as of this writing, are schemes for the S-3 Viking, P-3 Orion, E-2 Hawkeye and the Naval Reserve's F-8 Crusader.

For the most part, the tri-color seems to have returned.

One of the earliest examples of the stylized application of the "ND" tail letter combination on a Douglas A-4C of VA-305 at Point Mugu, California in 1971. Trim color is Light Green on fin and rudder, codes are Black. (B R Jackson)

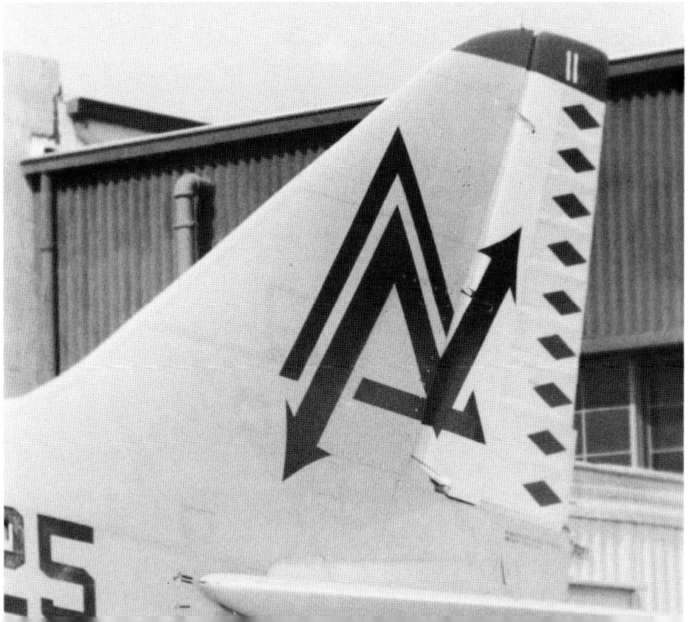

VA-25 A-7E Corsair II shortly after completion of 1972-73 West Pac Cruise. VA-25 Corsair IIs now carry series five numbers to match trim color of Light Green. Lightning bolt is Insignia Red with Orange Yellow circle and squadron designator in Red. (VA-25)

Light Blue and Medium Blue F-4J of VX-4 at Point Mugu in 1973. Camouflage was experimental. (B R Jackson)

Close-up of air intake showing small 'danger' warning sign. (B R Jackson)

Close-up of tail markings shows unusual application of squadron designation, which is included in data block in place of the aircraft model designation. (B R Jackson)

Grumman F-14A Tomcats of VF-2 contrast standard USN camouflage scheme and experimental Ferris scheme during 1976-77 Western Pacific Cruise of ENTERPRISE (CVN-65). (Tailhook Association)

INTO THE 80'S AND BEYOND

As of this writing, a highly detailed Military Standard covering all Navy and Marine Corps aircraft insignia, markings and paint schemes is being evaluated by all concerned agencies. The purpose of this document is to standardize the paint scheme and application of naval insignia and markings. The new document consolidates five military specifications and one military standard dealing with separate items and supersedes them.

The requirements for paint schemes and markings include size, color and approximate locations. Shown in forty-eight different aircraft illustrations, they vary with differences in configuration, type of aircraft and designated mission. The standard also provides a mechanism to obtain approval for deviation from the listed requirements. This military standard, as yet unserialized, carries the project number **F-82-20** and is dated 18 March 1983.

World conditions, being what they are, seems to justify and explain why the paint schemes on the Navy's aircraft has lost all its glory. Camouflage for concealment may seem somewhat out of place in today's super-sophisticated technological world but the possibility still exists that some Navy or Marine pilot somewhere, sometime, may encounter a weapons system operating on its visual back-up system or a visually directed gun system being operated from deep within some remote jungle or mountainous area.

The Air Combat Survivability Branch of the Naval Air Systems Command is always working on better ways to increase the combat survivability of the pilots and aircraft of the United States Navy and Marine Corps. Who knows what's coming next?

A-4E attached to 'Topgun' fighter tactics school at NAS Miramar, California. Tactical schemes were being formulated at this time. 3 September 1978 (Robert L Lawson)

A-7 Corsair II of Alameda's VA-304 with the stylized "ND" tail code in April of 1983. Scheme and markings are still 'Hi-Viz' even though the tactical scheme was authorized twenty months earlier. (Douglas R Tachauer)

VA-97 A-7E Corsair IIs on 19 June 1982 at NAS Lemoore the colorful markings then on their way out. (Jerry Kishpaugh)

Lockheed S3A Viking (159770) of VX-1 at NAS Patuxent River, Maryland on 26 September 1981 carries the new Tactical paint scheme. Top colors are FS 35237 and 36375 over FS 36495 under surfaces. (Douglas R Tachauer)

Lockheed P3C Orion (157326) of VX-1 at NAS Patuxent River, 26 September 1981. Tail letters are "JA", which are barely visible on top of rudder. Top colors are FS 35237 and 36375, with an underside of FS 36495. Both the S3A and P3C tactical scheme were experimental at this time. (Douglas R. Tachauer)

Vought A7E of VA-94 at NAS Lemoore during October of 1983. The Insignia White has been removed from the underside of this Corsair II, but markings are not as subdued as the final Tactical A7 Corsair II scheme which had been approved twenty months earlier. (Douglas R Tachauer)

VA-97 A-7Es on 19 June 1982 at Lemoore after being repainted in the new Tactical scheme. (Jerry Kishpaugh)

VC-12 TA-4J Skyhawk at NAS Oceana in October of 1982. Tactical scheme is carried with upper surface colors of FS 36320 and 36375 over underside color of FS 36495. This scheme was approved for the Skyhawk on 25 August 1980. (Douglas R Tachauer)

Reserve F-4S Phantom II of VF-302 from NAS Miramar in April of 1983. The Tactical scheme is carried, with a small stylized "ND" is painted in White on the rudder. (Douglas R Tachauer)

McDonnell F-4N Phantom II (152226) of VF-171 (Key West Detachment), NAS Oceana in October of 1982. Fin flash is Insignia Red. The national insignia on the underside of the starboard wing is out of proportion, the rectangles being too long. (Douglas R Tachauer)

F-4S Phantom II (155767) of VF-171 from NAS Oceana, 2 October 1982. Very small "AD" tail code can be seen at top of vertical fin. Topside colors are FS 35237 and 36320 over underside color FS 36375. This scheme was approved on 3 February 1982. (Douglas R Tachauer)

Douglas TA-4J Skyhawk (153516) of VF-43 at NAS Oceana in October of 1982. (Philip A Tachauer)

VF-43 F-5E (160793) in shades of Blue and Gray at NAS Oceana on 2 October 1982. (Douglas R Tachauer)

Northrop TF-18A Hornet (161355) of VFA-125 at NAS Lemoore in October of 1983. Strike Fighter Squadron One Two Five is the F/A-18 Hornet Fleet Readiness Squadron at Lemoore and carries the Tactical scheme approved on 30 July 1980. Top color is FS 36375 and bottom color is FS 36395. Anti-glare panel is FS 35237. (Douglas R Tachauer)

F-18A Hornet (161710) No 302 flown by Cdr Craig Langbehn, Executive Officer of Strike Fighter Squadron One One Three, (VFA-113) 'The Stingers', the Navy's first Hornet squadron. VFA-113 began training with the Hornet in March of 1983. (Douglas R Tachauer)

THE UNITED STATES COAST GUARD

After 28 December 1945, when the US Coast Guard again became part of the United States Treasury Department, and Coast Guard aircraft immediately began shedding its Navy warpaint in favor of the more visible search and rescue markings.

Basically the color of the aircraft was either NS Insignia White or Aluminum varnish. In some cases the air/sea rescue markings were applied over the basic camouflage tri-color scheme. Wing tips and floats of seaplanes were painted Glossy Orange Yellow with a 6 inch Glossy Black border separating the Glossy Orange Yellow from the basic color scheme of the airplane. A Glossy Orange Yellow fuselage band was applied between the empennage and the trailing edge of the wing. A Glossy Orange Yellow rectangle was placed immediately aft of the bow located national insignia, with the last three digits of the airplane's Bureau Number placed within.

The center section of the wing above the fuselage was painted Glossy Orange Yellow, and extended from approximately 6 inches outboard of the left engine to approximately 6 inches outboard of the right engine. The station name and last three digits of the Bureau Number were placed within this Glossy Orange Yellow area, as was the word RESCUE.

Coast Guard aircraft not engaged in air/sea rescue work, generally sported an overall Aluminum color and carried the words US COAST GUARD on the aft fuselage. The letters USCG appeared on the underside of the port wing as well as the topside of the starboard wing. Slight variations occurred, and it was not until 1951 that a uniform set of instructions was issued for USCG aircraft.

COAST GUARD PAINTING AND INSTRUCTIONS MEMORANDUM NUMBER 7 - 51 18 JUNE 1951

When the Commandant of the Coast Guard issued this painting document, it cancelled out seven older USN directives which were being used as reference.

Fixed wing landplanes were to be left generally unpainted, except that all surfaces, other than aluminum or its alloys, were to be given a coat of Aluminum pigmented finish. Landplanes could be painted Aluminized lacquer if the condition of the bare metal surfaces indicated signs of minor corrosion or to improve its appearance.

Seaplanes were to be painted Aluminized lacquer; this included amphibians.

Rotary wing aircraft (helicopters) were to be painted Glossy Orange Yellow. Rotor blades were to be painted Aluminum lacquer, and blade tips were painted identifying colors. (Same as USN helicopter blade tips of the period).

Anti-glare areas on Coast Guard aircraft were Non-Specular Black, as opposed to the NS Medium Green color used on Navy and Marine Corps airplanes.

Coast Guard markings for fixed wing aircraft consisted of the national insignia being applied to the right wing. The national insignia was also applied to both sides of the fuselage or vertical fin.

The letters USCG were to be applied in Glossy Black to the top side of the right wing and the underside of the left wing. The lettering was to read from inboard toward the wing tip. The words US COAST GUARD were to be applied in Glossy Black on both sides of the fuselage or hull.

The Coast Guard insignia was applied to each side of the fuselage or hull in the vicinity of the pilot's compartment.

The Coast Guard model and serial number was to be applied in Glossy Black on both sides of the vertical fin. The partial serial number of the aircraft was to be applied in Glossy Black to both sides of the fuselage or hull, utilizing the last four digits only, except in the case where only three had been assigned, in which case all three were to be applied. In addition, the partial serial number was to be applied to both sides at the nose or bow of the aircraft.

Rotary winged aircraft had the national insignia applied to both sides of the aircraft's fuselage.

The letters USCG were to be applied in Glossy Black to the underside of the helicopter's body or tail cone with the tops of the letters to the left side.

The words US COAST GUARD were to be applied in Glossy Black on both sides of the fuselage or tail cone.

The Coast Guard insignia was to be located on both sides of the fuselage.

The model and serial number were to be applied in Glossy Black on each side of the fuselage or tail cone.

A partial serial number was to be applied in Glossy Black to both sides and on top of the fuselage, using the last four digits only. If only three digits were assigned, then they were used in their entirety.

Helicopters with a tail rotor were to apply a Red warning arrow forward of the disc of the rotor with the words DANGER KEEP AWAY stenciled for safety purposes. The shaft of the arrow was to be centered as specified. The word DANGER was to be spaced above the shaft while the words KEEP AWAY were to be located similarly below the shaft.

SEARCH AND RESCUE AIRCRAFT

All helicopters, and the following aircraft, were considered to have as their primary mission, search and rescue.

PBM-5G
PBY-5AG
JRF-5G
UF-1G

Upper and lower surfaces of both wing tips were to be painted Glossy Orange-Yellow from the tip inboard approximately seven percent of the span (excluding span increased by the wing tip float). This area was to be extended inboard by a Glossy Black border of 6 inches.

A Glossy Orange Yellow band was to encircle the fuselage forward of the horizontal stabilizer. This band was to be 18 inches in width of JRF aircraft and 36 inches on others, and was to be enclosed by two 3 inch or 6 inch Glossy Black borders respectively. The aft edge of the band, including the border was to be approximately 9 and 18 inches respectively, forward of the leading edge of the horizontal stabilizer.

This scheme continued in use throughout 1951, 1952 and 1953. It would be a few more years before another major directive covering USCG aircraft would be issued, but when it came, Coast Guard airplanes would be the most

(Below) Coast Guard P4Y-2G Privateer from USCG Air Station, San Francisco, California in March 1954. The Overall Aluminum scheme of fixed wing landplanes with Orange Yellow rear fuselage band and Medium Green anti-glare panel is carried. (USCG)

distinctive and colorful of any aircraft in the sky.

In 1958, steps were taken to develop a new *easy-visibility* paint scheme for Coast Guard aircraft.

Many variations were tried with the most promising being the use of Fluorescent Blaze Orange, outlined in Black appearing on the nose of the aircraft, in a band around the aft fuselage and on the tail on a basic field of Insignia White paint.

Because of the inability of fluorescent paints to withstand sun and foul weather, a more durable type of paint was soon developed, and by 1960 Coast Guard aircraft were sporting Hi-Visibility schemes of International Orange, Black and Insignia White.

COAST GUARD 1967

In 1967, the Coast Guard began implementing the scheme in use today.

The overall scheme remained Insignia White, but the International Orange color was changed to a special shade called Coast Guard Red 40.

A diagonal stripe of Coast Guard Blue 41, was added to the aircraft's fuselage in the area aft of the cockpit cabin.

Detailed instructions covering paint patterns for this new scheme were covered in a series of large drawings which illustrated the paint scheme for each aircraft type.

Instructions for the application of the new scheme were contained in **Aviation Technical Note 2-68** of 3 May 1968.

A supplement to **ATN-2-68** was issued on 19 October 1970, under the title **ATN-2-68A**. No changes relative to the basic scheme were included, and it is mentioned here purely as reference.

Lockheed HC-130B Hercules from Barbers Point, Hawaii in 1963. International Orange replaced Fluorescent Blaze Orange due to the latter's inability to withstand the rigors of flight, weather, etc. Top of wing carries Black USCG lettering and US national insignia on Orange Yellow panels inboard of the International Orange panels near wing tip. (USCG via T E Doll)

Chicago, Illinois based Sikorsky HH-52A SeaKing illustrates the paint scheme as detailed in Coast Guard drawing 475-8-2 of 31 May 1968. Large fuselage stripe is Coast Guard Red (No 40), small stripe is Coast Guard Blue (No 41). Fore and aft colors are also Red (No 40) with balance of helicopter painted Insignia White. (Eric Lundahl via Harry Gann)

US Coast Guard Sikorsky HH-3F flying over Lake Pontchartrain, Louisiana in April of 1969. This is an excellent example of the Coast Guard paint scheme for this type aircraft. (USCG via Jim Sullivan)

(Left) Lockheed HC-130B Hercules with the revised USCG scheme brought into use in 1967. The USCG insignia is applied over a wide stripe of Coast Guard Red (No 40), immediately followed by a stripe of Insignia White followed by a stripe of Coast Guard Blue (No 41). (USCG via T E Doll)

US Coast Guard HU-25 from Sacramento, California on 1 May 1983. Base color of the aircraft is Insignia White with a wide fuselage stripe in Coast Guard Red (No 40) followed by a narrow fuselage stripe in Coast Guard Blue (No 41). Vertical tail surfaces feature Coast Guard Red (No 40). Lettering is Black. (Jerry Kishpaugh)

MOST COMMONLY USED FEDERAL STANDARD 595a COLORS

Light Blue	15102
Insignia Blue	15044
Light Green	14187
Olive Drab	14087
Light Yellow	13655
Aircraft Cream	13594
International Orange	12197
Insignia Red	11136
Maroon	10049
Insignia White	17875
Aircraft Gray	16473
Engine Gray	16081
Black	17038
Strata Blue	15045
Glossy Sea Blue	15042
Instrument Black	27038
Light Gray*	36440 (Used in Tactical Scheme)
Sea Gray	36118
Intermediate Blue	35164
Azure Blue	35231
Sky	34424
Interior Green	34151
Medium Green	34079
Dark Gull Gray	36231
Orange Yellow	13538
Mid Gray	36375 (Used in Tactical Scheme)
Light Gray	36495 (Used in Tactical Scheme)
Dark Blue Gray	35237 (Used in Tactical Scheme)
Unnamed Gray**	36320 (Used in Tactical Scheme)

**Light Gray 36440 was called Light Gull Gray prior to 1 July 1971. The reason for the Color name duplication with 36495 is unknown.*

***FS Color number 36320, which is used in the Tactical Scheme, is a shade of Gray that, at this writing, has not yet received a name.*